CULTURES OF THE WORLD
Slovakia

Cavendish Square
New York

Published in 2021 by Cavendish Square Publishing, LLC
243 5th Avenue, Suite 136, New York, NY 10016

Library of Congress Cataloging-in-Publication Data

Names: Gottfried, Ted, author. | Nevins, Debbie, author.
Title: Slovakia / Ted Gottfried, Debbie Nevins.
Description: Third edition. | New York : Cavendish Square Publishing,
   [2021] | Series: Cultures of the world | Includes bibliographical
   references and index.
Identifiers: LCCN 2020012569 (print) | LCCN 2020012570 (ebook) | ISBN
   9781502655936 (library binding) | ISBN 9781502655943 (ebook)
Subjects: LCSH: Slovakia--Juvenile literature.
Classification: LCC DB2711 .G68 2021 (print) | LCC DB2711 (ebook) | DDC
   943.73--dc23
LC record available at https://lccn.loc.gov/2020012569
LC ebook record available at https://lccn.loc.gov/2020012570

Editor, third edition: Debbie Nevins
Designer, third edition: Jessica Nevins

The photographs in this book are used with the permission of: cover © Martin Jancek/Moment/Getty Images; p. 1 kunmingzijin/Shutterstock.com; p. 3 Attila Csipe/Shutterstock.com; pp. 5, 62 Halfpoint/Shutterstock.com; p. 6 Peter Hermes Furian/Shutterstock.com; p. 7 Rosalicka/Shutterstock.com; p. 8 leonov.o/Shutterstock.com; p. 10 Solanika/Shutterstock.com; p. 12 Jacek Jacobi/Shutterstock.com; pp. 13, 49, 83 Leonid Andronov/Shutterstock.com; p. 14 Rastislav Sedlak SK/Shutterstock.com; pp. 15, 19 Jan_S/Shutterstock.com; p. 16 saiko3p/Shutterstock.com; p. 17 Niks Freimanis/Shutterstock.com; p. 18 Uhryn Larysa/Shutterstock.com; pp. 20, 81 Peter Vanco/Shutterstock.com; p. 21 Pecold/Shutterstock.com; p. 22 Gelia/Shutterstock.com; p. 24 Peter Jurco/Shutterstock.com; pp. 26, 27 Popperfoto via Getty Images/Getty Images; p. 28 Universal History Archive/Universal Images Group via Getty Images; p. 29 Keystone/Hulton Archive/Getty Images; p. 30 Bettmann/Getty Images; p. 32 LUBOMIR KOTEK/AFP via Getty Images; pp. 33, 34 David Brauchli/Sygma via Getty Images; p. 36 Andrej Balaz/Shutterstock.com; p. 38 Martyn Jandula/Shutterstock.com; pp. 40, 120, 128 Ventura/Shutterstock.com; p. 42 Alexandros Michailidis/Shutterstock.com; p. 46 KarSol/Shutterstock.com; p. 50 Pe3k/Shutterstock.com; p. 51 Anna Jedynak/Shutterstock.com; p. 54 Viliam.M/Shutterstock.com; p. 56 krolya25/Shutterstock.com; p. 57 Michal Blaho/Shutterstock.com; pp. 58, 119 Renata Sedmakova/Shutterstock.com; p. 60 Marcel Jancovic/Shutterstock.com; p. 63 katarinag/Shutterstock.com; p. 64 Marek Valovic/Shutterstock.com; p. 65 agilard/Shutterstock.com; p. 66 Julia Schoenstaedt/SOPA Images/LightRocket via Getty Images; p. 68 Mario Kramar/Shutterstock.com; pp. 70, 126 Jan Danek jdm.foto/Shutterstock.com; p. 71 Kiev.Victorv/Shutterstock.com; p. 72 Landscape Nature Photo/Shutterstock.com; p. 73 Sergiy Palamarchuk/Shutterstock.com; p. 76 Borisb17/Shutterstock.com; p. 78 Geothea/Shutterstock.com; p. 79 rorem/Shutterstock.com; p. 82 Richard Semik/Shutterstock.com; p. 84 vidalgo/Shutterstock.com; p. 86 Arsenie Krasnevsky/Shutterstock.com; p. 89 graphia/Shutterstock.com; p. 91 kmn-network/iStock Editorial/Getty Images Plus; p. 92 Frans Sellies/Moment/Getty Images Plus; p. 94 Nataliia Sokolovska/Shutterstock.com; p. 96 Nick Fox/Shutterstock.com; p. 97 Lubos K/Shutterstock.com; p. 98 amnat30/Shutterstock.com; p. 99 Michal Knitl/Shutterstock.com; p. 100 lennystan/Shutterstock.com; pp. 101, 112, 122 Jaroslav Moravcik/Shutterstock.com; p. 102 VeronikaV/Shutterstock.com; p. 103 kennymax/Shutterstock.com; p. 104 David Lodge/WireImage/Getty Images; p. 106 Radu Cadar/Shutterstock.com; p. 108 Borshchevskyi Oleg/Shutterstock.com; p. 110 Kayo/Shutterstock.com; p. 111 phototravelua/Shutterstock.com; p. 113 tramper79/Shutterstock.com; p. 114 Pepiccino/Shutterstock.com; p. 116 Beneda Miroslav/Shutterstock.com; p. 124 SweetHour/Shutterstock.com; p. 127 Zeedoherty/Shutterstock.com; p. 130 noxnorthys/Shutterstock.com; p. 131 Valeria Vechterova/Shutterstock.com.

Some of the images in this book illustrate individuals who are models. The depictions do not imply actual situations or events.

CPSIA compliance information: Batch #CS20CSQ: For further information contact Cavendish Square Publishing LLC, New York, New York, at 1-877-980-4450.

Printed in the United States of America

Find us on

CONTENTS

SLOVAKIA TODAY

SLOVAKIA IS NOT SLOVENIA. THAT'S ONE OF THE FIRST THINGS the citizens of this country want to make clear right off the bat to geography-challenged foreigners. For its part, the country of Slovenia is equally anxious not to be confused with Slovakia, though the two do share some similarities. Both countries are located in Central Europe, and both derive their names from the Slavic peoples who settled in the region many centuries ago. Both Slovakia and Slovenia were also once part of larger 20th-century communist nations that fell apart following the dissolution of the Soviet Union in 1991.

Slovakia once made up one half of the nation of Czechoslovakia, which existed in different guises from 1918 to 1993. Slovenia, which is farther south in Central Europe, was a part of the much larger federation of Yugoslavia, but that's another story. In the collapse of those big national entities, smaller countries emerged, seeking independence and identity. Slovakia was one of them.

That's another thing Slovaks would like foreigners to know. Slovakia is not half of anything. It is now a whole, independent country unto itself. It separated from its "other half," now the Czech Republic, in the poetically dubbed "Velvet Divorce" of 1993.

This map shows Slovakia; its capital, Bratislava; and its important cities, rivers, and lakes. It also shows parts of the five nations that border the country.

Even through their 75 years of national union, the Czech and Slovak cultures never truly homogenized into one, and those long-simmering tensions finally pulled them apart.

Slovakia, therefore, is a relatively young country, but its history and culture are old. A landlocked state surrounded by the nations that once occupied or annexed it, Slovakia is a realm of castles and mountains. The people are religious, conservative, and proud of their heritage. They tend toward traditional speech patterns, customs, and folkways. Their reserved nature toward visitors often conceals a uniquely Slovak warmth and humor. The culture is rich with folk arts, architectural treasures, abundant natural beauty, and culinary bounty.

Times change, however, and Slovakia is changing along with them. After enduring an authoritarian regime in its first years of independence, the country has been trying to align more firmly with democratic Western Europe. To that end, it successfully joined the European Union (EU) in 2004. However, the path to democracy is never easy, and once achieved, it is tough to hang on to. Slovakia has been struggling with corruption in the upper ranks, which has gone hand-in-hand with the nationalist, populist politics that have overshadowed its journey to democracy.

The issue broke open in 2018 with the sensationalistic and scandalous murder of journalist Jan Kuciak and his fiancée. Kuciak had been investigating the corrupt activities of businessman Marian Kocner and his associates, with their alleged ties to the government then in power. The investigation revealed a vast network of corrupt government officials, judges and other court officials, police, businesspeople, journalists, and even assassins. Kuciak's murder galvanized the public, which took to the streets in droves to protest such criminal treachery.

The subsequent trial, which is still ongoing as of spring 2020, exposed shocking revelations. It also figured largely in the 2019 election of President Zuzana Caputova, a progressive liberal, and in the 2020 parliamentary electoral

A photo of the slain couple Jan Kuciak and Martina Kusnirova is posted in a public park in Bratislava in March 2018. The inscription says, "We will not forget."

losses of the ruling party. However, the primary gains of that election went to conservative populist parties, which distrust the EU and advocate for more restrictive policies toward migrants, women, and the press, and in matters concerning gender and sexual identity issues.

While Slovaks grapple with what kind of nation they wish to be, however, the economy is generally doing well. Also, if statistical evaluations are to be believed, Slovakia has become happier in recent years. The World Happiness Report is a landmark survey by the United Nations Sustainable Development Solutions Network. It reports on the state of global happiness, ranking countries by how happy their citizens perceive themselves to be.

The World Happiness Report 2020 found that Slovakia's overall happiness quotient for the period 2017—2019 came in at number 37 out of 153 countries. That falls below that of the United States at number 18 and its former other half, the Czech Republic, at number 19. In this report, the happiest nation overall was Finland at number 1 and the least happy was Afghanistan.

A happy couple treks near Slovakia's Popradske Pleso glacial lake in the snowy High Tatras.

The good news for Slovakia is that it is trending upwards. On a scale of 0 (unhappy) to 10 (happy), Slovakia rose from a score of 5.97 in 2013, for a ranking of 46th happiest country in the world, to a 6.28 in 2020, or 37th in the world. That's a significant improvement.

There are numerous other statistical evaluations of the world's nations on topics of happiness, peace, civil liberties, press freedom, and economic freedom. Slovakia tends to fall in similar categories across the board. Such reports reveal a country that is doing well but not great. All in all, though, the trend for Slovakia tends to be toward the better. It struggles to overcome corruption, as already mentioned; hostility toward ethnic minorities, migrants, and refugees; and an aging population, with the problems that entails. Slovakia still needs to significantly improve its transportation infrastructure, its underfunded health and education sectors, and the lack of economic opportunity in the poorer eastern part of the country.

Whether it will find continued democratic and economic success or succumb to corruption, nationalism, and more restricted freedom remains to be seen. Corruption appears to be the main factor holding the country back. Some analysts say 40 years of communism trained Slovaks to accept and even admire corruption. The best laws don't matter if they are not enforced.

President Caputova summed it up in February 2020: "[It's as] if we have forgotten that democracy ... is mainly about the spirit of freedom, of justice, tolerance, and solidarity. These are bound together by the rule of law." For a country with so much to offer, the stakes couldn't be higher.

GEOGRAPHY

Lomnicky Peak in the High Tatras retains its icy glaciers while flowers bloom near a mountain lake in the summertime.

1

S LOVAKIA IS A MOSTLY mountainous, landlocked country in Central Europe. For much of the 20th century, it was one half of Czechoslovakia, a nation that has since broken up. Its former other half, the Czech Republic, is now its neighbor.

Its other neighbors are Poland to the north, Ukraine to the east, Hungary to the south, and Austria to the southwest. The Czech Republic (also called Czechia) borders Slovakia to the northwest; the two share a border of 150 miles (241 kilometers).

Slovakia occupies a total area of 18,933 square miles (49,035 square kilometers)—almost the size of Vermont and New Hampshire together. Slovakia's average elevation is 1,503 feet (458 meters) above sea level, with some portions of the country rising significantly higher.

Slovakia's high terrain descends into lowlands that meet the Danube River, which forms part of the country's 390-mile (627 km) border with Hungary. Meanwhile, the Eastern Slovak Lowland defines the southeastern part of the country, which borders Ukraine for 60 miles (97 km). These fertile agricultural regions lie in pastoral contrast to the rugged peaks that define most of Slovakia.

MOUNTAINS

Slovakia is dominated by the Carpathian Mountains, a chain of peaks that begins at the Danube Gap near Bratislava, the nation's capital, and

• • • • • • • • • • • • •
Bratislava is the only capital city in the world that borders two other countries—in this case, Austria and Hungary. The point where the three countries meet is in an empty field about 5.6 miles (9 km) from the city center. The spot is marked with a concrete post from the old barbed-wired "Iron Curtain" that used to run along this border, separating communist Czechoslovakia and Hungary from Austria and the rest of free Western Europe.

Mountain flowers shimmer against the background of Gerlach Peak in the High Tatras.

continues in a wide arc into Eastern Europe, ending in Romania. The section that runs through Slovakia is called the Western Carpathians.

The High Tatras are a geologic division of the Carpathians that covers northern Slovakia and extends into Poland. The highest peak in Slovakia, at 8,711 feet (2,655 m), is Gerlachovsky Stit (GEHR-la-HUL-shkee SHTEET), or Gerlach Peak. The High Tatras include 29 peaks higher than 8,200 feet (2,500 m). High Tatras National Park is one of nine national parks in Slovakia.

Below the High Tatras, in central Slovakia, are the Low Tatras, which rise between the valleys of the Vah River to the north and the Hron River to the south. The highest peak of the Low Tatras is Dumbier at 6,703 feet (2,043 m), which lies in Low Tatras National Park.

The Slovak Ore Mountains are another part of the Western Carpathians, extending across south-central Slovakia for about 90 miles (145 km) from

Zvolen to Kosice. They are particularly known for their high-grade iron ore, as noted in their name. The famous Dobsinska Ice Cave is found in this region.

RIVERS

The mountain crags of the Low Tatras melt into hills and lowlands in the southern part of Slovakia, and dense forests give way to fertile farmlands. Here, the mighty Danube River (Dunaj) flows past the capital city of Bratislava and runs along the border with Hungary.

Starting in the High Tatras, the Vah (VACK) River—Slovakia's longest waterway, at 270 miles (434 km)—joins the Danube at the town of Komarno, flowing on from there to the Black Sea. The Slovak part of the Danube runs 107 miles (172 km), making it the sixth-longest waterway in the country. Slovakia has many other rivers as well, with the others in the top five being the Hron (the second longest), the Ipel, the Nitra, and the Hornad. All of these

This aerial view shows the Vah River at Trencin in Slovakia.

Since 1975, the United Nations Educational, Scientific and Cultural Organization (UNESCO) has maintained a list of international landmarks or regions considered to be of "outstanding value" to the people of the world. Such sites embody the common natural and cultural heritage of humanity and therefore deserve particular protection. The organization works with the host country to establish plans for managing and conserving their sites.

The 900-year-old Spis Castle sits atop a hill in eastern Slovakia.

UNESCO also reports on sites that are in imminent or potential danger of destruction and can offer emergency funds to try to save the property.

The organization is continually assessing new sites for inclusion on the World Heritage list. In order to be selected, a site must be of "outstanding universal value" and meet at least one of ten criteria. These required elements include cultural value—that is, artistic, religious, or historical significance—and natural value, including exceptional beauty, unusual natural phenomena, or scientific importance.

As of January 2020, there were 1,121 sites listed: 869 cultural, 213 natural, and 39 mixed (cultural and natural) properties in 167 nations. Of those, 53 were listed as being "in danger."

Slovakia has five cultural sites and two natural ones. Both natural sites are shared with—or extend into—other European countries. They are the Ancient and Primeval Beech Forests of the Carpathians and Other Regions of Europe, a transboundary property that is found in Slovakia and 11 other countries; and the Caves of Aggtelek Karst and Slovak Karst, found in Slovakia and Hungary. The cultural sites are the Bardejov Town Conservation Reserve, the Historic Town of Banska Stiavnica, Levoca (a historic town) and Spis Castle, Vlkolinec (a mountain village), and the Wooden Churches of Slovakia's Carpathian Mountain Area.

rivers flow south and eventually join the Danube, sometimes by way of other, larger rivers.

SEASONS AND CLIMATE

Generally speaking, the seasons of Slovakia are rigorous, and sometimes cruel. The winters are cold and bitter, with freezing temperatures. Rainfall can be heavy in summer, particularly in June and July. In the High Tatras, summer temperatures can verge on freezing.

The kindest weather is found in the lowlands in springtime. However, even there the balminess is offset by rainfall, which is good for crops but bad for tourism. Most spectacular are the autumn storms in the highlands, when thunder rebounds off the mountainsides and sudden lightning illuminates an otherworldly vista.

Cars try to navigate a snowy road in the town of Lomnica, in the High Tatras.

Bratislava Castle and Saint Martin's Cathedral dominate the red-roofed city of Bratislava.

REGIONS AND CITIES

Slovakia is divided into eight regions. Each has the same name as the city that is its capital. The regions are Bratislava, Trnava, Nitra, Trencin, Zilina, Banska Bystrica, Presov, and Kosice.

BRATISLAVA   The city of Bratislava, capital of Slovakia, is in the southwestern part of the country, spanning both banks of the Danube River. Only 34 miles (55 km) from Vienna in Austria, it is a jarring mixture of Baroque architecture, communist-era high-rise apartment buildings, and the sprawling outskirts of

CAVES

Some of Slovakia's most astounding natural sights are hidden underground. The country has more than 2,400 caves, only a few of which are open to the public. Some are ice caves, where ice formations create an otherworldly variety of icicles, stalagmites, columns, and even frozen waterfalls. These include Demanovska Ice Cave in the Low Tatras and Dobsinska Ice Cave in Slovak Paradise National Park.

Visitors admire the subterranean sights in the Dobsinska Ice Cave.

Dobsinska is a part of the UNESCO World Heritage site called the Caves of Aggtelek Karst and Slovak Karst. This site consists of more than 1,000 caves that extend over (or under) the border of Hungary and Slovakia. Three of the site's seven cave systems are in Slovakia.

The caves were formed in a karst landscape. That geological term describes a topography in which rainwater seeping into soluble bedrocks has slowly dissolved them. The process creates sinkholes, underground rivers and streams, caves, and springs. Karst landscapes are often made of limestone and other soft rocks like dolomite and gypsum.

This particular concentration of caves is unusual not only because of its astonishing beauty, but also because it displays the extremely rare combination of tropical and glacial climatic effects. From a scientific standpoint, this exceptional feature makes it possible to study geological history over tens of millions of years.

Only 1 percent of the cave area is open to the public and is visited by around 300,000 people each year.

construction projects that never seem to be finished. However, appearances can be deceiving; the central city is cheerful and culturally exciting, with excellent museums, art galleries, and music of every variety.

Once a first-century Celtic settlement, today Bratislava has a population of about 435,000. Restoration efforts have included the re-cobbling of ancient streets and the refurbishing and repainting of historic buildings. The ultramodern Eurovea complex, slated to feature Slovakia's first skyscraper upon completion, embodies the city's new spirit of development.

KOSICE   The administrative center of eastern Slovakia, Kosice (ko-SHEET-sah) is a hub of industry, science, commerce, and culture. The entire Kosice region encompasses 2,607 square miles (6,753 sq km) and has a population of nearly 800,000 people. The city of Kosice itself has a population of around 240,000. It dates back to 1230 CE, and its historic center is known as the Urban Heritage Area because of its reconstructed main street lined with the mansions and palaces of well-off merchants from a variety of eras. Saint Elizabeth's Cathedral

The State Theater of Kosice is the focus of this view of Main Street in the center of Kosice.

is considered one of the most beautiful Gothic structures in the world. It is the city's oldest landmark, built between 1378 and 1508, and features an altar with 3 magnificent statues and 48 panel paintings.

BANSKA BYSTRICA In central Slovakia, the district of Banska Bystrica (BAHN-skah BIS-trit-sah) is notable for the number of protected natural sites it encompasses, including Low Tatras National Park, which at 313 square miles (811 sq km) is the largest such natural area in Slovakia.

One of Slovakia's most popular tourist destinations, Banska Bystrica offers both winter and summer facilities. In the cold-weather months, there are many ski resorts for both alpine and cross-country skiing, as well as bobsled trails and lakes and ponds for ice-skating and ice fishing. During summer, there are resorts devoted to swimming and boating, as well as the area's famous thermal baths.

The cultural hub of central Slovakia, the city of Banska Bystrica is notable for its architecture, with its impressive churches and municipal buildings.

People stroll through the main square in Banska Bystrica on a summer day.

"Hashtag Trnava" artwork livens up a pedestrian area in the city. In the background is the Renaissance Town Tower, and farther back, the spire of the Church of the Holy Trinity.

NITRA The region of Nitra (NYI-tre) sits on a low plain, separated from Hungary to the south by the Danube River. In addition to the city of Nitra, it includes the river port of Komarno, a trading hub for all of Europe. The area covers 2,450 square miles (6,343 sq km) and includes the two nature reserves of Zobor, both of which are famous for their plant and animal life.

The city of Nitra is one of the oldest settlements in Slovakia and had been both the bishopric of the Great Moravian Empire and the site of the first Christian church in the country. It offers a rich cultural life, and there are regular exhibitions and concerts by artists and musicians from all over Europe.

TRNAVA Sometimes called the Slovak Rome, Trnava (TER-ne-ve) in western Slovakia is perhaps the most intellectual of Slovakia's regions. A center for religious study in the 13th century, the city has had a university since the 17th century. The region is known for its mineral springs and medicinal baths. The well-known spa resort at Piestany is only 22 miles (35 km) from the city.

TRENCIN The district of Trencin (tren-CHEEN), in the valley of the Vah River, is one of the more pastoral areas of Slovakia. With a climate more temperate than most of the country, its green, wooded trails are a popular destination for hikers. Racehorses are bred in the district, and horseback riding is a favorite activity. The city, originally a Roman military colony, is guarded by a fortified castle dating back to the 11th century.

ZILINA The region of Zilina (ZHIL-en-ah), located in the Low Tatras, has some of the world's most famous caves. It adjoins Poland to the north and the Czech Republic to the west, and it is made up of heavily forested valleys surrounded by mountains.

Not only spelunkers (cave explorers) but also hunters and fishing enthusiasts are drawn to the region. The local dams—Oravska Priehrada and Liptovska Mara—have made the local rivers, the Vah and the Kysuca, ideal for water sports.

The city of Zilina, the fourth largest in Slovakia, stands where the rivers meet, and its famous 16th-century Renaissance belfry, Burian's Tower, looms over them.

PRESOV The High Tatras are the site of both the district and city of Presov (PRESH-awf). Here, within view of both Poland and Ukraine, the snow-capped mountains offer breathtaking vistas of natural beauty. In the north of the area are two fortified castles from the Middle Ages: Saris and Kapusany. In the south, the elliptically shaped city of Presov is partially surrounded by fortifications and dozens of Renaissance-style homes. The town square is known for the 200-year-old Neptune Fountain, with its classical statuary.

The Neptune Fountain stands near the Cathedral of Saint Nicholas in Presov.

INTERNET LINKS

https://www.slovakia.com/regions
This travel site provides a look at the eight regions of Slovakia.

https://whc.unesco.org/en/statesparties/sk
This is the World Heritage page for Slovakia's seven listings.

https://www.worldatlas.com/geography/slovakiageography.htm
This overview of Slovakia's geography includes maps.

HISTORY

The ruins of Devin Castle stand on a high cliff over the Danube and Morava Rivers near Bratislava.

2

SLOVAKIA IS A FAIRLY NEW COUNTRY, but it's also a very old one. Its history reads like a terrible dream filled with warfare, hardship, and subjugation. To awaken from such a nightmare is to embrace joy and liberation. For Slovaks, this awakening is nationhood.

Archaeological evidence indicates that in the centuries before 1000 BCE, various nomadic tribes of Slavic origin settled, moved on from, and resettled areas of present-day Slovakia. In the fifth century BCE, the Illyrians and later the Celts established more permanent settlements. These groups were expelled by Germanic conquerors in 100 BCE. Attempts by the Roman Empire to dislodge the Germanic peoples were unsuccessful.

However, a mass infiltration by Slavs reached its peak in the fifth century CE. By the sixth century, Slavs had overrun the area, and in 623, Slavic tribes united under the warrior Samo and established supremacy over the region.

EMPIRE AND RELIGION

Territories of present-day Slovakia were annexed by the Great Moravian Empire in 833 CE. Great Moravia was the first important West Slavic state in Central Europe, founded by Slavic tribes that would later be known as Czechs and Slovaks. The empire encompassed areas that are today central and western Slovakia, the Czech Republic, and parts of Hungary, Poland, and Germany. Lasting only a little more than 70 years, it nevertheless established civilization and religion in the area with lasting effects.

Devin Castle, one of the oldest in Slovakia, dates to the year 864 CE, and possibly earlier. Parts of it were added on over the centuries, up through the 17th century. The castle has witnessed a great deal of history, including its destruction at the hands of Napoleon in 1809. Now partially renovated, the castle is a museum and a tourist attraction.

In 863, Cyril and Methodius, Christian missionaries from Thessalonica in present-day Greece, implemented a successful program of Christianization that established the religious identity of the territory of Slovakia, which has lasted to the present time. Determined that the Bible should be accessible to converts, Cyril created the first Slavic alphabet and translated the Bible into the language of the people.

The Great Moravian Empire, however, became destabilized. There were murmurings of revolt and plots. Hostile Hungarian forces massed on the borders. The Moravian prince sat uneasily on his throne. Finally, the Great Moravian Empire fell apart in 907. In 1018, the Slovak region was absorbed into the Magyar (Hungarian) Empire. Slovakia would continue to exist as a part of this empire for nearly 1,000 years.

A bronze statue of Prince Pribina stands in Nitra, Slovakia. Pribina was the first ruler of Slavic origin to accept baptism and to build a Christian church.

GERMAN COLONIZATION

As part of the Hungarian Empire, the territory of present-day Slovakia enjoyed a certain amount of prosperity. A mining industry was established, and Slovak earth gave up profitable amounts of gold, silver, and copper. Trading relations were established with other countries, and exports of fur and amber resulted in a surplus that enriched the Slovak economy.

In 1237, however, savage Tatars invaded from the east, and the economy fell into a major depression. In an effort to drive out the Tatars and rebuild the economy, the rulers of Hungary recruited Saxon-German artisans to settle underpopulated areas of the Slovak region. It was the beginning of a German migration that eventually established them as the majority population in many mining towns.

In the 14th century, Matus Cak, a charismatic warlord, led a rebellion against royal power. Establishing Trencin as a capital, he and his forces controlled much of the country until his death in 1321, when Hungary reestablished control. In 1514, Juraj Doza led an army of 50,000 peasants in a second rebellion against

Hungary, which was brutally put down. There followed a successful invasion of Hungary by Turkey. The former Hungarian capital was moved from Buda (Budapest) to Bratislava. In 1686, the Turks were driven out in a series of notoriously bloody battles.

MAGYARIZATION

The formation of the Austro-Hungarian monarchy under the House of Habsburg in 1867 was both a blessing and a curse for Slovaks. Serfdom was abolished, and a school system for all Slovak children was established. However, much of the reform was undercut by a program of enforced Magyarization (Hungarianization), aimed at replacing the Slovak culture and language with Hungarian equivalents.

By 1907, Hungarian had become the only language permitted in Slovak schools. Protests by Slovak intellectuals at the systematic attempt to destroy their ethnic identity were squelched. As a result, a movement of both Slovaks and Czechs, who were also being subjected to Magyarization, formed to oppose Austro-Hungarian domination. This was the beginning of the push for an independent Czech-Slovak nation.

When World War I broke out in 1914, Slovak men were called up to serve in the Austro-Hungarian army. Many rebelled, and some joined with Czechs to form guerrilla units whose activities tormented the Austro-Hungarian forces. Meanwhile, during the war, there was a diplomatic campaign waged by Slovak and Czech nationalists to persuade the United States, Great Britain, and France to support the liberation of their lands from Austria-Hungary.

The result was that at the end of the war, Slovakia announced its independence from the empire and its incorporation into the independent nation of Czechoslovakia.

BETWEEN THE WARS

In October 1918, Tomas Garrigue Masaryk, a leading advocate of Czech independence, was elected president of the new Republic of Czechoslovakia. The region of Slovakia was still mainly a countryside of small farms. Programs

Jozef Tiso, shown here in 1939, was a Catholic priest and a Slovak nationalist leader who became president of the Slovak Republic in 1939.

to establish an industrial base were initially successful, but in the 1920s, mismanagement by Czech bureaucrats undermined them. A movement for a separate Slovak nation began to gain momentum.

The worldwide Great Depression of the 1930s hit Czechoslovakia very hard. The Slovak region suffered close to 50 percent unemployment. Opposition to the federal government in Prague was bitter and growing. The movement for the Slovaks to secede and go their own way was gaining popularity. Agitating for an independent Slovak nation, in the 1935 national Czechoslovakian election, communist and right-wing groups received 60 percent of the Slovak vote.

During this period, Czechoslovakia was plagued with problems. Among the area's large German population, groups of Nazi sympathizers were organizing. Speeches by the German leader Adolf Hitler repeatedly laid claim to the Czechoslovakian area known as the Sudetenland, located in Bohemia and part of Moravia. Once briefly part of Germany, the Sudetenland had a large German population. The Germans of the Slovak region supported Hitler's right to annex the Sudetenland.

WORLD WAR II

In 1938, over the protests of the Czechoslovakian government, Great Britain and France signed the Munich Agreement with Hitler, ceding the Sudetenland to Germany. They believed that such sacrifice would appease Hitler and avoid a war. However, as history demonstrates, Hitler was not appeased. In March 1939, as German troops advanced from the Sudetenland to invade the remainder of Bohemia and Moravia, and as Hungary, Germany's ally, occupied an area of the southern Slovak region, the Slovaks officially separated from Czechoslovakia and declared Slovakia an independent nation.

The Slovak People's Party (SLS)—also called Hlinka's Slovak People's Party after its founder, Andrej Hlinka—took control of the new nation, and the party's leader, Jozef Tiso, a Catholic priest, became, in effect, the dictator of Slovakia.

Tiso and the SLS had strong ties to the Nazis of Germany and immediately proved to be very much in sympathy with their policies. Strong censorship rules patterned after those of Nazi Germany were enforced. All political parties except the SLS were banned. Political opponents were jailed, and their families were persecuted. A Jewish Code was implemented, and about 75,000 Jews were rounded up and transported to Nazi concentration camps, where they were killed.

The Hlinka Guards of the Slovak People's Party display Nazi armbands in 1939.

Resistance to Tiso and the Slovak Nazis built slowly within Slovakia. In 1944, the Slovak National Uprising (SNP) finally revealed the wide extent of opposition to the Tiso regime. The SNP was led by units of the former Slovak army and included many partisan groups that had been acting against the Nazis since the start of World War II. The SNP was so effective that Tiso was forced to call on German troops to deal with it, and even then it took two months to suppress the uprising.

In March 1939, Jozef Tiso, the leader of Slovakia, was summoned to Berlin for a meeting with German leader Adolf Hitler, also known as the Führer. Tiso was told that Hungarian troops massed on the Slovak border would invade unless Hitler took over the protection of Slovakia. Tiso replied that he hoped the Slovaks would "prove themselves worthy of the Führer's benevolence." Subsequently, the Treaty of Protection (Schutzvertrag), making Slovakia

Jozef Tiso meets with Adolf Hitler, the leader of Nazi Germany, in 1939.

a satellite of Nazi Germany, was signed. Immediately, anti-Semitic restrictions were imposed on the Jewish population.

Not counting those living in Slovak lands that had been annexed by Hungary, there were about 90,000 Jews (3 percent of the population) living in Slovakia in 1940. A two-pronged policy to Aryanize Jewish property and to isolate Jews from the general population was instituted. The policy was dictated by the German Nazis and carried out by Tiso and the Slovak People's Party, familiarly known as Hlinka. The Hlinka Guard was a militia maintained by the Slovak People's Party from 1938 to 1945; it functioned as Slovakia's state police and helped implement Hitler's policies.

Within a year, 10,025 Jewish businesses were liquidated, and 2,223 were transferred to Aryan ownership. Three large labor camps—Sered, Vyhne, and Novaky—were built, and able-bodied Jews were herded into them. In the autumn of 1941, a special order was enforced to clear Bratislava of Jews. They were sent to labor camps to join other Jews.

In February 1942, the Slovak government asked the German government for assistance in removing all Jews from Slovakia. The Germans complied, charging the Slovaks a fee for each Jew deported. At first, only males who were able to work were expelled, but when the Slovaks protested that families should not be broken up, the Germans agreed to include women and children in the mass deportation. They had to reassure the Slovaks that the Jews would never return and that no claims would be raised against stolen Jewish property. Between March 26 and October 20 in 1942, 60,000 Jews were sent to the Auschwitz concentration camp in the Lublin area of Poland to be put to death.

A Jewish woman (*right*) wears a badge with a capital Z (for *Zidovsk*, or "Jewish") under the Nazi regime in Slovakia in 1939.

Giuseppe Burzio, a Roman Catholic archbishop in Slovakia, protested. He wrote to the Vatican in Rome, calling Tiso demented. The Vatican sent a message that the death trains must stop. Pope Pius XII personally intervened. Finally, the deportations were temporarily halted. In 1944, however, around 5,000 Jews involved in the Slovak National Uprising were taken prisoner. Slovakia was now occupied by German troops, and 13,500 more Jews were deported to the death camps.

Russia's Red Army liberated Slovakia in April 1945. Tiso was tried for treason, convicted, and executed. He had shared responsibility for the killing of about 75,000 Slovak Jews—83 percent of the Jewish population in the Slovak region.

PRAGUE SPRING

At the close of World War II, in pursuit of the retreating German Nazi army, Soviet troops overran Czech and Slovak lands. Czechoslovakia was reestablished as a nation after the war, and Slovakia was once again a part of it. Communists backed by the Soviet Union took over the Czechoslovakian government in February 1948. The country's administration was once again centralized in Prague, to the detriment of Slovakia.

Many Slovak nationalists and others opposed Communist Party rule. They were dealt with harshly. Disappearances, torture, forced labor, and executions were common over the next two decades. In 1968, Slovak Alexander Dubcek became the Communist Party leader. The Soviet secret police (KGB) reported to Moscow that Dubcek had counterrevolutionary tendencies and would pursue policies unacceptable to the Soviet Union.

On August 26, 1968, a young Czech woman shouts at Soviet soldiers sitting on tanks in the streets of Prague, Czechoslovakia.

Dubcek introduced a policy that he called "socialism with a human face." It set out democratic reforms such as political opposition, freedom of the press, and freedom of speech. There were public protests about the methods of the Soviet police and the beatings and torture in the labor camps. Citizens demanded an end to Soviet domination of their country. That period of restored freedoms is known as the "Prague Spring." A Czechoslovakian revolution was stirring.

MOSCOW PUTS ITS FOOT DOWN

The Soviet Union stopped it. On August 20, 1968, a massive airlift dropped several hundred thousand troops and tanks into Czechoslovakia. Soviet planes filled the skies over Prague. Dubcek gave in to the Soviet demands. Democratic reforms were scrapped. The major radio station in Prague was silenced. All political parties besides the Communist Party were outlawed. People who weren't hard-line Communist Party devotees were excluded from the government. The media were put under Soviet control. Soviet troops were permanently stationed in Czechoslovakia.

Dubcek was removed from power and replaced by another Slovak, Gustav Husak. The reform movement was effectively dead, and there followed a stagnant period in which a dreary status quo defined Czechoslovakian politics. Many professionals and other educated civilians were forced to earn their living doing menial jobs. That was followed in the 1980s by economic and political stagnation, corruption of the state system, and severely lowered living standards. Prior to World War II, Czechoslovakia had enjoyed the 10th-highest standard of living in the world. By the end of the 1980s, it had plunged to 42nd place, well below many developing nations.

In March 1988, Soviet premier Mikhail Gorbachev discarded the Brezhnev Doctrine, a policy that allowed the Soviet Union to intervene in the affairs of other countries if they deviated from communist principles. This was the policy the Soviets had used to justify their occupation of Czechoslovakia. This signaled a new opening for Czechoslovakian protest.

THE VELVET REVOLUTION

Toward the end of 1989, the citizens of Czechoslovakia began expressing strong discontent with the Communist Party regime. The first of several demonstrations took place on August 21, 1989, the 21st anniversary of the crushing of the Prague Spring. The demonstrators—a mix of young and old, intellectuals and laborers—sang the national anthem and waved the national flag as they demanded freedom of expression, thought, association, and belief. Censorship had controlled all aspects of their lives. They wanted the freedom to decide what music to play and what books to read without fear of government reprisal.

On November 17, 1989, the anniversary of the death of nine students killed by the Nazis in 1939, Prague's youth organized an officially sanctioned demonstration in Wenceslas Square in Prague. The students declared an indefinite strike and were joined by actors and musicians. Although it was a peaceful protest, riot police were sent in to suppress the students. As a

Students shout their support of Vaclav Havel for the presidency during a 1989 protest rally at Wenceslas Square in Prague.

result, a week of demonstrations followed in Prague in which, in a city of 2 million, more than 750,000 people participated. On November 27, 10 days after the student strike, a general strike was held; over half the population stopped working for two hours.

The strike precipitated the resignation of the chairperson of the Federal Assembly and heralded the collapse of the Communist Party government. On December 29, 1989, the dissident playwright Vaclav Havel was elected president, Vaclav Klaus was elected prime minister, and Alexander Dubcek became the speaker of parliament. This period of change came to be called the "Velvet Revolution" because there were no casualties.

Moscow's restraint this time around was a sign of its own internal crisis. By 1991, the Soviet Union itself would collapse, and communism—at least in Europe—with it.

Slovak politician Vladimir Meciar addresses the press on January 1, 1993, the day Slovakia became an independent nation once again.

THE VELVET DIVORCE

Among the Slovaks, however, another sort of revolution was brewing. The question of an independent Slovakia still hung over the country. The Slovaks had long resented their treatment as second-class citizens. Those sentiments were fueled by the Slovak politician Vladimir Meciar, a strong supporter of complete independence for Slovaks. In 1992, negotiations over a new federal constitution for Czechoslovakia were deadlocked. Meanwhile, an independent Slovak parliament voted for independence and elected Meciar as prime minister. Czech prime minister Klaus agreed and insisted on separation.

President Havel resigned in protest, refusing to preside over the split. Finally, on January 1, 1993, the Czechoslovakian federation was dissolved, and the independent Republic of Slovakia was established. The Czech portion of the former nation, for its part, became the Czech Republic, or Czechia. In the first few months of independence, relations between the two republics were determined by 25 interstate treaties that provided a framework for issues such as the division of property, federal institutions, and a common currency.

A SLOVAK NATION

Western Europe and the United States were quick to grant diplomatic recognition to independent Slovakia. However, the leftist policies of Meciar and his authoritarian style of government sent the Slovak economy into a tailspin. In March 1994, a parliamentary vote of no confidence removed him from office. A coalition government was formed, but a majority partnership of right-wing and left-wing parties once again named Meciar as prime minister.

At this time, the parliament authorized the sale of enterprises that had been state-owned during the Communist Party rule of Czechoslovakia. Meciar canceled such sales and halted all efforts to privatize Slovakia's industries. He imposed penalties and threatened the closure of all newspapers and television

Controversial prime minister Vladimir Meciar returns to his post in 1994.

and radio stations that criticized the government. In effect, he returned Slovakia to an autocratic leadership that adopted the restrictions and policies of communism. Slovakia was criticized by US president Bill Clinton and cited as a violator of citizens' rights by many human rights organizations.

The 1998 elections ousted Meciar as prime minister. He was replaced by Mikulas Dzurinda, leader of the right-wing Slovak Democratic Coalition (SDK). Dzurinda was faced with problems of an unstable economy, high unemployment, and ethnic tensions involving the Hungarian and Roma populations. In an attempt to return to power, Meciar decided to run for president in the 2004 election. Eleven candidates ran in the first round, on April 3. Only two candidates could advance to the second round. The contenders were Vladimir Meciar and Ivan Gasparovic. The latter won with close to 60 percent of the vote, and Gasparovic was inaugurated on June 15, 2004.

That same year, Slovakia was admitted to NATO and to the European Union (EU), two organizations that, in many ways, essentially define Western Europe. In 2009, Slovakia adopted the euro, further aligning with the EU. During this first decade of the 21st century, Slovakia sent a strong signal that its allegiance from then on would be to the democratic West as opposed to Russia.

That allegiance would be tested in the events of the following years. Conservative politicians gained ground. Prime Minister Robert Fico, who served from 2006 to 2010 and again from 2012 to 2018, tried to steer a middle course between EU interests and building a good relationship with Russia. He was not always successful; for example, in 2014, unlike most Western leaders, Fico refused to criticize Russia's annexation of the Crimean Peninsula, which was Ukrainian territory.

Fico was also vocal in his dislike of Slovakia's Roma minority. Also, in 2015, when Europe was facing an unprecedented wave of refugees and economic migrants fleeing war, violence, and poverty in the Middle East and Africa, he opposed the EU's plan to settle the displaced people among its member states. He refused to take in any migrants, particularly Muslims. "Islam has no place in Slovakia," he said, adding that his government "monitors every single Muslim in Slovakia."

The North Atlantic Treaty Organization, or NATO, is a mutual defense alliance of 29 member countries from North America and Europe. Formed in 1949 in opposition to communism and the Soviet Union, it has since expanded to include several formerly communist nations, including Slovakia.

The European Union (EU) is a political and economic organization of 27 European member nations.

On February 21, 2018, Jan Kuciak and his fiancée, Martina Kusnirova, were shot and killed in their home in Velka Maca, Slovakia. It was no random murder. Kuciak, 27, was an investigative reporter for the online news site Aktuality.sk and had been reporting on high-level tax evasion and fraud. At the time of his murder, he had been focused on suspicious activity regarding a notorious businessman named Marian Kocner, who was alleged to have deep ties to organized crime.

Kocner was immediately suspected of involvement in the killings. For one thing, Kocner had phoned Kuciak and threatened him, which the journalist then reported to the police. The police, however, took no action. In his last, unfinished article, Kuciak detailed how certain people with ties to organized crime had spent years embezzling European Union funds intended for the development of eastern Slovakia, a relatively poor region of the country. Those alleged criminals were known to have connections to certain high-ranking Slovak government officials.

As news of the murders became public, Slovaks responded with shock and took to the streets in mass protests. The demonstrations sparked a political crisis between Prime Minister Robert Fico and President Andrej Kiska that ultimately resulted in Fico and his cabinet members resigning in March 2018.

Police arrested Kocner and seven other people in connection with the murders; one of them cooperated with police, naming Kocner specifically. The trial of Kocner and three of his associates began in January 2020, and was unresolved as of spring 2020.

Protesters in Bratislava on March 2, 2018, carry a banner saying "An attack on journalists = an attack on us all."

Fico resigned in 2018, following the Jan Kuciak murder scandal, and Peter Pellegrini assumed the role of prime minister. Following the 2019 elections, the politician, lawyer, and environmental activist Zuzana Caputova became the president. In 2020, Pellegrini lost his post as prime minister to Igor Matovic of the populist, right-wing Ordinary People Party. The next elections are scheduled for 2024.

A populist political party or politician holds the view that the common person is oppressed or ignored by the powerful "elite" and that government needs to be wrested away from those in charge. Populists believe they alone represent "the people," whom they tend to define as those who agree with them politically.

INTERNET LINKS

https://www.bbc.com/news/world-europe-44873067
This article explains the involvement of 'Ndrangheta, an Italian organized crime group, in the Kuciak murder, and in Slovakia in general.

https://www.nytimes.com/2019/03/14/world/europe/slovakia-jan-kuciak-kocner.html
The Kuciak murder and the events that followed are the focus of this article.

https://www.thoughtco.com/the-velvet-divorce-1221617
The dissolution of Czechoslovakia is explained on this page.

https://time.com/5730106/velvet-revolution-history
This article examines Czechoslovakia's Velvet Revolution of 1989.

https://www.wilsoncenter.org/event/no-saint-jozef-tiso-and-the-holocaust-slovakia
This brief article looks at the Slovak leader Jozef Tiso's complicity in the Holocaust.

GOVERNMENT

The Planet of Peace Fountain is outside the Grassalkovich Palace, the residence of Slovakia's president.

3

SLOVAKIA IS A PARLIAMENTARY republic, a multiparty representative democracy in which the people choose their government. In this political system, the people elect representatives to the legislature, or parliament. Those representatives, in turn, select the head of government—typically a prime minister along with his or her cabinet ministers— according to party strength as expressed in the elections. The parliament also votes on legislation, or the laws of the nation.

The government is established in the constitution. It lays out the form, structure, powers, and duties of the government. The document also codifies the rights and responsibilities of the people, as spelled out in the laws of the land.

THE CONSTITUTION

The Constitution of the Slovak Republic dates to the time when Czechoslovakia broke apart into two separate nations. September 1, 1992, the day the new constitution was passed, is now celebrated in Slovakia as Constitution Day, a national holiday.

In Slovakia, suffrage is universal, and the voting age is 18. Citizenship is not by birth but only by descent. At least one parent must be a citizen of Slovakia.

On September 1, 2019, the Slovak flag is raised in celebration of Constitution Day in Bratislava.

The document provides for equality for all, regardless of creed or belief, financial status, gender, language, nationality, origin, parentage, political party, race, religion, skin color, or social status. It provides for freedom of assembly, association, expression, movement, opinion/thought/conscience, the press, and religion. Also, it spells out a long list of rights, protections, and prohibitions.

Among those rights are the right to health care, as expressed in Article 40, which states, "Every person shall have the right to protect his or her health. Through medical insurance, the citizens shall have the right to free health care and medical equipment for disabilities under the terms to be provided by law." Article 44 says, "A person shall have the right to a favorable environment," and goes on to spell out a citizen's duty to protect the environment.

Among the prohibitions are censorship, capital punishment (the death penalty), and torture. Article 41, which was entered as an amendment in 2014,

Many, but not all, national constitutions begin with a preamble, or introduction. More than just pretty words, it typically sets the tone for the nation itself and the document to follow. A look at the preamble to Slovakia's constitution reveals how that is accomplished:

> We, the Slovak People
> Bearing in mind the political and cultural heritage of our predecessors, the experience gained through centuries of struggle for our national existence, and statehood,
> Mindful of the spiritual bequest of Cyril and Methodius, and the historical legacy of Great Moravia,
> Recognizing the natural right of nations to self-determination,
> Together with members of national minorities and ethnic groups living in the Slovak Republic,
> In the interest of continuous peaceful cooperation with other democratic countries,
> Endeavoring to implement democratic forms of government, guarantee a life of freedom, and promote spiritual, cultural and economic prosperity,
> We, the citizens of the Slovak Republic, have, herewith and by our representatives, adopted this Constitution:

A preamble often begins by identifying who is speaking—in this case, the "Slovak People." It also usually explains the motivation for creating the document. Here, it is "to implement democratic forms of government ... and economic prosperity."

Along the way, it is typical to refer to the history that brought the nation to where it is today. Here, the lines beginning with "Bearing in mind" and ending with "Great Moravia" do exactly that, mentioning "our predecessors" and the "centuries of struggle" for independence and self-determination. The preamble also establishes a national identity—who are we?—making a point here of including minority groups. For the roots of that identity, the preamble harkens back to the people's Christian spiritual heritage (Cyril and Methodius) and their Slavic ancestral land (Great Moravia).

Finally, a preamble also typically spells out the nation's ideals. This one mentions democracy, "self-determination," "continuous peaceful cooperation" with other nations, "a life of freedom," and "prosperity."

The president of the Slovak Republic, Zuzana Caputova, appears at a press conference in Brussels, Belgium, on June 25, 2019.

establishes marriage as a "unique union between a man and a woman," thereby prohibiting, though not mentioning, same-sex marriage.

The document has been amended several times since its writing, most recently in 2017. Amendments to the constitution require three-fifths of the votes in the parliament to pass.

THE EXECUTIVE BRANCH

Slovakia, like most parliamentary republics, has both a president and a prime minister, both of whom make up the executive branch of the government, along with the cabinet of ministers. The president is the head of state—the formal head of the nation—but has limited powers. The people elect the president directly by popular vote. The prime minister is the head of government and holds the most power. The prime minister is elected indirectly, as described previously, by the political party that has won the most seats in parliament.

In 2019, Zuzana Caputova became the president of Slovakia. She is to serve a five-year term, after which she will be eligible to run for a second term. Caputova is the first woman to serve as the nation's president, as well as the youngest person, at age 45 when elected, to hold the position. A lawyer by profession, she is known as a progressive politician with a special interest in environmental activism.

In 2018, Peter Pellegrini became the prime minister following the resignation of Robert Fico in the wake of the Jan Kuciak murder and scandal. Pellegrini had previously held other positions in the government and was the deputy prime minister at the time of Fico's leaving. As of December 2019, he also took the post of minister of health.

On February 23, 2020, just days before the nation's parliamentary elections, Pellegrini was hospitalized with a sudden illness, sparking rumors that he had contracted the dreaded coronavirus that was rapidly spreading worldwide at the time. That allegation was denied, but in any event, Pellegrini and his party were defeated in the election by the center-right opposition party Ordinary People (OLANO), which took 25 percent of the vote and won 53 seats in the 150-seat parliament. The party's leader, Igor Matovic, used unconventional tactics—publicity stunts—in his campaign, which focused on combating corruption.

THE LEGISLATIVE BRANCH

The parliament is a unicameral, or one-house, body called the National Council (Narodna Rada). It consists of 150 members who are elected every four years by popular vote. A number of political parties participate, and they are represented in the National Council in proportion to the number of votes they receive. The minimum requirement to be seated is 5 percent of the popular vote. The last election was in 2020, so the next one will be in 2024.

THE JUDICIAL SYSTEM

The breakup of Czechoslovakia left Slovakia with an outdated judicial system riddled with injustices and heavily weighted against the individual in favor of the state. Immediate reforms were adopted, based on the Austro-Hungarian codes of justice. However, this was put in place at the same time as the policies of privatization of state-owned industries and creation of a small business economy. The judicial system, including judges, prosecutors, and lesser functionaries, was inevitably involved in this, and politics, not justice, was often the deciding factor in the decision-making process.

In 2002, the parliament passed legislation that created a Judicial Council. This 18-member body includes the Supreme Court chief justice and a variety of presidential and parliamentary appointees who serve five-year terms with a maximum of two terms. The council is responsible for the nomination of judges, who are vetted for competence and ethics. All judges except those of the Constitutional Court are appointed by the president from a list proposed by the Judicial Council. Judges appointed through this process serve for life, but they can be removed at age 65 at the discretion of the president. The Judicial Council is also responsible for holding disciplinary hearings in cases of judicial misconduct.

RATING DEMOCRACIES

Any country may call itself a democracy, but how well does the description fit the reality? In some cases, there's quite a wide gap between the high-minded words in a nation's constitution and the actuality. It all depends on how well a government functions to protect democratic principles. Several international organizations watch closely to evaluate how well the world's governments are doing on that score.

Freedom House *is a US-based independent watchdog organization that conducts research and advocacy on democracy, political freedom, and human rights. In its annual "Freedom in the World" report, it ranks nations on such matters and assigns a finding of "free," "partly free," or "not free."*

In its 2019 report, it held a relatively bright view of freedom in Slovakia, classifying it as "free," with an aggregate score of 88 out of 100. For comparison, the United States scored a bit lower, at 86, though it still earned the rank of "free." Finland, Norway, and Sweden all earned a perfect score of 100, while Syria came in last, with a "not free" score of 0.

The Economist Intelligence Unit (EUI) *Democracy Index 2019 came to a somewhat different conclusion. The EIU is a London-based research and analysis company affiliated with the news magazine the* Economist. *It evaluates 167 countries on 60 indicators, scoring each between 0 and 10, in which 10 is best. Using the aggregate score, it then classifies a country as a "full democracy," a "flawed democracy," a "hybrid regime," or an "authoritarian regime." In its 2019 report, Slovakia ranked 42nd, with an overall score of 7.17, putting it in the category of "flawed democracy." The report pointed to the Jan Kuciak murder and its apparent government connections as one reason.*

For perspective, the Czech Republic came in a bit higher but was still classified as "flawed." It ranked at number 32, with a score of 7.69. The United States that year also fell into the "flawed" category, coming in at number 25, with a score of 7.96. Norway ranked number 1, with a "full democracy" score of 9.87. Not surprisingly, North Korea came in last, at number 167, an "authoritarian regime" with a score of 1.08.

Both evaluating reports agreed that the overall state of global democracy was in decline in 2019.

There are 55 district courts and 8 regional courts in Slovakia. The regional courts function as courts of appeal and also hear certain cases of overriding national importance. There is a Supreme Court and a Constitutional Court as well. The Supreme Court is the highest judicial authority in the country. It only hears cases that have first been tried in a regional court. It can annul decisions or send cases back to regional courts for a rehearing.

The Constitutional Court is an authority independent of the judicial system. As its name implies, it is set up to ensure that judicial decisions are in compliance with the Slovak constitution. Unlike other judges, members of the Constitutional Court are chosen by the entire Slovak parliament, with approval from the president. They serve for 12-year terms.

INTERNET LINKS

https://www.cia.gov/library/publications/the-world-factbook/geos/lo.html
The *CIA World Factbook* provides up-to-date information about Slovakia's government.

https://www.constituteproject.org/constitution/Slovakia_2014 .pdf?lang=en
The online Constitution Project presents a PDF of Slovakia's constitution in English.

https://freedomhouse.org
Freedom House annually reports on the state of democracy in Slovakia in its "Freedom in the World" report.

https://www.prezident.sk
This Office of the President site is in Slovak only but can be translated.

The 1 euro coin shown here represents the currency of much of the European Union, including Slovakia.

4

I N THE YEARS FOLLOWING ITS 1993 "Velvet Divorce" from the Czech Republic, Slovakia got off to a slow start. Historically, Slovakia had always been the less industrialized and less developed part of Czechoslovakia. Now on its own, the country was held back by the authoritarian regime of Vladimir Meciar and high levels of corruption. Following the 1998 elections, though, a new government adopted economic reforms in anticipation of joining the European Union, and things improved considerably. Indeed, the economy boomed so strongly that from 2000 to 2008, the Slovak economy was referred to as the "Tatra Tiger." (The name Tatra comes from the country's Tatra mountain range.)

Slovakia's market-based economy is driven largely by automobile and electronics exports. The country has attracted a significant amount of foreign investment due to its relatively low-cost yet skilled labor force, and its geographic location in the heart of Central Europe. This infusion

In 2004, Slovakia joined the European Union, along with the Czech Republic, Poland, Hungary, Lithuania, Latvia, Estonia, Slovenia, Cyprus, and Malta. In 2009, Slovakia adopted the euro as its currency, further aligning with the EU.

Gross domestic product (GDP) is a measure of a country's total production. The number reflects the total value of goods and services produced over one year. Economists use it to determine whether a country's economy is growing or contracting. Growth is good, while a falling GDP means trouble. Dividing the GDP by the number of people in the country determines the GDP per capita (per person). This number provides an indication of a country's average standard of living—the higher the better.

In 2017, the GDP per capita in Slovakia was approximately $33,100. (However, the International Monetary Fund forecast for the country's 2021 GDP per capita was much improved, at an estimated $41,094.) The 2017 figure is considered medium-high, and it ranked Slovakia 61st out of 229 countries listed by the CIA World Factbook. For comparison, the United States that year was number 19, with a GDP per capita of $59,500. The Czech Republic was number 47, with $35,500, and Slovakia's other neighbors ranked as follows: Austria did best, ranking at number 31, with a GDP per capita of $50,000; Hungary was 68th, with $29,600; Poland was 69th, with $29,600; and Ukraine ranked very low, at number 146, with only $8,800.

of capital has produced jobs and a correspondingly low unemployment rate, and it has fueled economic growth.

AGRICULTURE

Although about 40 percent of the land in Slovakia is used for agriculture, the sector contributes only 3.8 percent of the nation's GDP. Roughly 3.9 percent of the Slovak labor force works on farms, which produce grains, potatoes, sugar beets, fruit, hops, dairy products, and meat products from cattle, pigs, and poultry. The southern part of Slovakia, which borders Hungary, is known for its rich farmland.

A major economic aim for the government is to increase the agricultural production of small farms rather than build up agribusinesses. The government views the regionally balanced development of agriculture as necessary to maintaining the rural population, which is essential to the cultural character of the country.

Privatization of collective farms initially increased the number of farmers dramatically, from 1,000 in 1991 to 19,720 in 1994. Since then, however, the agriculture sector has been shrinking for several reasons. Many farmers practice subsistence farming on small farms. Their methods are outdated and inefficient. Farmers are also getting older. Fewer young people are interested in going into farming as a career. The work is poorly compensated and seen as having low value in society. To counter that trend, the Ministry of Agriculture and Rural Development began subsidizing young farmers who were starting their own operations.

However, land ownership is an obstacle to those who want to farm. The land itself is fragmented into a multitude of extremely small parcels, which are stuck in a quagmire of uncertain ownership and shady lease agreements. In addition, a large portion of Slovakia's land is under foreign ownership. Some of it was purchased on speculation and sits idle. Slovakia passed laws requiring residency and agricultural production on such land, but they were at odds with EU requirements and had to be abolished.

Straw bales on a wheat field make for a charming sight in Slovakia.

MANUFACTURING

A Skoda auto retailer in Nitra, Slovakia, sells brands owned by the Volkswagen Group. Skoda was founded as a Czech automobile manufacturer but now is part of Volkswagen.

Throughout the 1990s, Slovakia struggled to stimulate a sluggish economy. After all, it came into independence having had some of the least effective state-run industries in Czechoslovakia. By the turn of the 21st century, however, things were looking up. The GDP jumped by about 4 percent, foreign investment totaled $1.5 billion, and there was a strong increase in exports. Slovakia was admitted into the international Organisation for Economic Co-operation and Development (OECD), an intergovernmental economic organization with 36 member countries that works to stimulate economic progress and world trade.

Bratislava, Kosice, and the towns along the Vah River are Slovakia's main manufacturing centers. Important industries include automobiles, machinery, steel, ceramics, chemicals, textiles, food and beverage processing, arms, and petroleum products. Of those, automobile manufacturing is the country's largest industry. In 2019, it accounted for 13 percent of Slovakia's gross domestic product and for 35 percent of its exports.

Slovakia has four automobile factories and in 2018 was the world's biggest per-capita car producer. That year, it produced 1,080,000 cars, making it the 7th-largest car producer in the EU and the 20th-largest in the world. Perhaps the most important company in the country is Volkswagen, which employs around 14,000 people around the country, including at its huge plant in Bratislava, making it Slovakia's largest private-sector employer. In 2017, Volkswagen Slovakia experienced its first-ever strike, which lasted only six days. It ended with a wage deal that gave workers the largest pay raise among Slovakia's carmakers, although they still earn less than Volkswagen's employees in Germany. Volkswagen Slovakia also produces Audis and Porsches.

Other cars manufactured in the country include Peugeot in Trnava; Kia Motors vehicles in Zilina; Jaguar Land Rover in Nitra; and the K-1 Attack Roadster, a sports car built by the Slovak company K-1 Engineering.

Slovakia has many attractions to lure visitors from other countries. Natural beauty and mountainous landscapes, historic castles and towns, luxurious health spas and thermal springs, and ski resorts are among its appealing features. In fact, the only big tourist attraction it lacks is a seashore. Slovakia can't do anything about that, but it can stress the charms of its many other temptations.

A hiker takes a photo of Strbske Pleso, a mountain lake in the High Tatras of Slovakia.

Bratislava, with its rich cultural life, and the mountains of the High Tatras, with their incredible views, are among the top destinations. However, skiers, cyclists, hikers, wildlife enthusiasts, and snowboarders can easily find many places for fun. Visitors can find tours of national parks, castles, palaces, churches, wineries, and the caves of the eastern region. The UNESCO World Heritage sites are also important tourist destinations, particularly the spectacular 900-year-old Spis Castle (Spissky Hrad), one of the largest medieval castle sites in Cental Europe.

During the Czechoslovakian era of communism, most tourists came from other communist nations in Eastern Europe. Independence has broadened Slovakia's appeal, although most visitors are still those from the immediate area—particularly the Czech Republic, Poland, and Germany. However, more and more, people are coming from farther afield. Indeed, in 2017, the seventh most common country of origin on the list of international tourists to Slovakia was China, with 61,346 visitors. That same year, 46,728 tourists came from the United States.

In 2018, the number of tourists, both domestic and foreign, in Slovakia reached 5.49 million. The number of international arrivals in 2017 (the latest available) was a record high of 2.16 million.

SERVICES

The service sector grew rapidly as Slovakia's economy boomed. In 2017, services made up 61.2 percent of the economy, and the percentage has likely grown since. Typically, countries with larger service sectors are considered more advanced than industrial or agricultural economies.

The service sector includes a broad range of economic activities that do not, in themselves, produce specific goods. Rather, these businesses offer services (hence the name), from house cleaning to ballet lessons to brain surgery to financial planning. People who make cars, for example, are in the manufacturing sector, but people who fix those cars are in the service sector. The service industry includes legal services; banking; architectural, engineering, and construction companies; accounting and advertising firms; telecommunications enterprises; the arts, entertainment, and recreation industries; social services such as health care and education; wholesale and retail businesses; railway and trucking firms; utility companies; and travel and tourism services.

Slovakia's service sector is dominated by trade and real estate. However, tourism, as an industry, is growing quickly in terms of both domestic vacationers and international visitors.

TRANSPORTATION

Slovakia's major cities are served by a variety of public transportation systems. Bratislava's buses, trams, and trolleybuses run frequently and connect the city with outlying towns. A national bus network serves most regions of the country with a regular schedule of transportation that is reliable at prices comparable to train fares. Bus travel is popular with Slovaks, as the buses are generally faster than the regional trains and run more frequently than the express train.

There are 2,225 miles (3,580 km) of Slovak railroads. The Bratislava-to-Kosice route (stopping at Zilina, Trencin, and Poprad) is covered in five hours. All express trains between Budapest in Hungary and Prague in the Czech Republic stop at Bratislava. There are also trains daily between Bratislava and Vienna, a trip of a little more than an hour. Much of Slovakia's in-country shipping is done by rail as well as by truck.

The road network of Slovakia extends over about 35,375 miles (56,930 km), providing access to all but the most mountainous wilderness areas of Slovakia. Most of the roads are paved, including 288 miles (464 km) of expressways. Snow removal is a high priority, and every effort is made to keep roads clear in the most severe winter weather.

Slovakia has no access to the ocean, but it has 107 miles (172 km) of navigable waterways, all on the Danube River. There are active river ports at both Bratislava and Komarno.

There are 35 airports in Slovakia, of which 19 have paved runways. Bratislava and Kosice are the two large international airports, with six smaller airports also servicing international flights. There are daily flights between the two cities. Flights from Bratislava regularly connect with all major European airports. The former flag carrier, Slovak Airlines, ceased operations in 2007. As of 2020, there is no Slovak national carrier. Slovakia also has a heliport.

INTERNET LINKS

https://www.cia.gov/library/publications/the-world-factbook/geos/lo.html
The *CIA World Factbook* has information on Slovakia's economy and transportation networks.

http://www.oecd.org/economy/slovak-republic-economic-snapshot
The OECD offers an up-to-date economic snapshot of Slovakia with other related data.

https://www.slovakia.com/top10
This Slovak travel site lists its top 10 attractions.

ENVIRONMENT

A view from a ridge in Low Tatras National Park looks out across a valley to a mountainous landscape.

5

I N GENERAL, SLOVAKIA HAS NOT BEEN at the forefront of environmental activism. Its approach to tackling environmental issues has been spotty and uninspiring, as it has tended to focus more on economic growth at the expense of greener initiatives. However, as a member of the EU, it is required to meet certain environmental standards, and it has been progressing, however unevenly, as it strives to meet those goals.

For example, the amount of pollutants in the nation's wastewater has been decreasing. Between 1995 and 2016, the number of pollutants diminished by almost 80 percent—thanks to the modernization of wastewater treatment plants, the implementation of more efficient purification processes, and the decline of industrial production in general.

On the other hand, while the percentage of the population that is connected to public sewer systems increased from 54 percent in 2007 to 66.4 percent in 2016, that figure is still unacceptably low. It falls below the average in international comparison. Wastewater management remains one of Slovakia's main challenges in environmental policy planning.

The country relies heavily on nuclear power, which generates around 54 percent of its energy, with the remainder coming from hydroelectric and traditional fuel sources. Slovakia has four nuclear reactors, with two new plants under construction. (Those have been repeatedly delayed, however, as their safety designs have been reevaluated. Neighboring Austria, in particular, has been fighting Slovakia's nuclear expansion.) Three older reactors were decommissioned after not meeting EU standards. Renewable energy sources (besides hydropower) account for just 6.8 percent of energy production.

In 2019, Slovakia launched a new environmental strategy, called Greener Slovakia. One of its goals is to extend the non-intrusive areas of its national parks by 50 percent by 2025 and by 75 percent by 2030. Mining will be prohibited.

The new initiative also looks to increase organic farming to at least 13.5 percent of the total agriculture sector (from 9.85 percent in 2018). Other "green" goals, such as a higher level of recycling of municipal waste and more emphasis on renewable energy sources, are also part of the plan.

FORESTS

Approximately 5 million acres (2 million hectares) of Slovakia—40 percent of the nation's land area—are forested. Like so much else, these forests suffered under the heavy industrialization of the communist era. When communism

Wood is harvested in the coniferous forests of the Tatra Mountains.

Approximately 40 percent of Slovakia is covered by woodlands, mostly beech and spruce trees and a rich variety of shrubs. To preserve this ideal habitat for wildlife, the Slovak government enforces laws for the protection of animals and imposes strict restrictions on hunting. Slovakia has also fought off the effects of acid rain and the encroachment of deforestation. Forests abound with all sorts of birds: pheasants, ducks, partridges, storks, wild geese, grouse, and avian predators such as eagles and vultures. Wild animals such as bears, wolves, and lynx are protected from hunters. In Low Tatras National Park, marmots, otters, and mink roam free in the woodlands. The chamois (shown here),

a mountain antelope, is an endangered species protected by law inside and outside Slovakia's parks. Once almost extinct, its numbers are now increasing, and repeated sightings have been reported by hikers.

collapsed in Czechoslovakia and the other countries of Eastern Europe, its shocking legacy was that large areas of forests were dying as a result of acid rain. In the hurry to build industrial societies that would equal those of the Western world, little attention had been paid to problems of pollution. Prevention and safety measures lagged far behind production.

Today, air pollution and acid rain continue to cause defoliation (the premature loss of leaves from trees) in parts of Slovakia's forests. Defoliation is the first step in deforestation (the dying out of trees in forests).

Nearly 50 percent of Slovak forests overlap with Natura 2000 sites. Natura 2000, a project of the European Union, is a coordinated network of protected lands in Europe—the largest such network in the world. It covers more than

Oil refineries operate in Bratislava.

18 percent of the EU's land area and nearly 6 percent of marine territory, and it exists to protect Europe's most valuable and threatened species and habitats.

Slovakia is still attempting to align its forest management policies with those of the EU. Such practices as clear-cutting and logging in primeval forest areas, for example, are considered environmentally harmful and threaten certain animal populations. According to the EU, the Slovak government has not, as yet, provided sufficient resources to implement the necessary conservation measures.

AIR POLLUTION

In 2015, the World Health Organization (WHO) reported that Slovakia had some of the most polluted air in Europe. The air was killing around 6,300 people in the country each year. In its 2019 report, the EU estimated that air pollution was leading to about 5,200 premature deaths in the country. Although emissions of various pollutants have decreased significantly in recent years, the quality of Slovakia's air is obviously still a matter of great concern. Among the steps the EU recommended to solve this problem is a reduction in the use of coal for domestic heating.

WATER POLLUTION

Just as Slovakia has an air pollution problem, it also has a water problem. Only about 56 percent of its bodies of water are reported to be in good condition. The Danube River is relatively clean running through Slovakia, which has been a signatory to the Danube River Protection Convention since 1994. Part of the reason for the Danube's good quality in Slovakia is that it first benefits from significant pollution protections while flowing through Austria.

Most of Slovakia's major rivers are in average condition, with the exception of the Nitra and Small Danube, which are the most polluted, according to the

Water Research Institute. Agricultural runoff is one problem, where pesticides and fertilizers run into the rivers. Untreated wastewater, another big source of pollution, seeps into rivers underground.

As the old threat from industrial waste has improved, however, new sources of concern have arisen. Plastic waste and microplastics, as well as pharmaceutical waste, are among the newest hazards threatening the Danube and other rivers in Slovakia, and indeed all of Europe.

INTERNET LINKS

http://www.oecd.org/environment/country-reviews/Mid-term -report-EPR-Slovakia-feb-2018.pdf
This 2018 OECD document is the second of three progress reports on Slovakia's environmental performance, the first having been in 2011, and the final report scheduled for 2021 or 2022.

https://spectator.sme.sk/c/20558626/environment-ministry -warns-of-underground-water-pollution-in-vrakuna.html
This article discusses the problem of underground water pollution in the Bratislava region.

https://www.theguardian.com/sustainable-business/2016/nov/13/ danube-looming-pollution-threats-worlds-most-international -river-microplastics-fertiliser
This article takes a broad look at the environmental threats to the Danube River.

SLOVAKS

A young Slovak woman models a traditional costume.

6

THE CITIZENS OF SLOVAKIA, regardless of their ethnicity, are Slovaks. There are no Slovakians; the term is not used. However, the word Slovak also refers to the majority ethnic group in the country. Slovakia is a fairly homogenous country—with a population of about 5,440,600 (in 2020), it's made up mostly of ethnic Slovaks. They account for 80.7 percent of the people.

Officially, Hungarians make up the largest minority group, at 8.5 percent. Roma (or Romani) people are said to account for 2 percent, but they may actually represent upwards of 7 to 11 percent of Slovakia's population. It's hard to say because the Roma are a transient group, moving both within the country and across its borders. They are also more likely to represent themselves as "other" rather than as "Roma" on documents because of prejudice. Therefore, census numbers probably underestimate the true number of that group.

There are also small pockets—each making up 1 percent or less of the population—of Czech, Ruthenian, Ukrainian, Russian, German, and Polish people living in Slovakia.

In the 21st century, the birthrate in Slovakia has been quite low, with 9.3 births per 1,000 people in 2020—making it number 203 out of 229 nations in the world. This translates to an average fertility rate of 1.44 children born per woman of reproductive age. Simply maintaining a population level requires a fertility rate of 2.1. The country's birthrate is therefore below a critical level, and the population numbers are falling.

LIFE EXPECTANCY

As is true in most countries, Slovak women tend to live longer than men. In the Slovak Republic, a baby girl born in 2020 could expect to live to be 81.6 years old, on average, if mortality factors remain the same in the future. A baby boy born the same year could expect to live 74.3 years. The average Slovak, regardless of sex, could thus expect to live 77.8 years. This statistic, called life expectancy at birth, is considered a prime indicator of a population's well-being and a measure of the overall quality of life in a given country.

This finding ranked Slovakia at 75th place in the world in 2020. For comparison, the Czech Republic scored higher that year, at 56th place, with an average of 79.3 years; the United States was number 45, with a combined life expectancy of 80.3 years.

AGING POPULATION

In the last two decades or so, the average age of Slovaks has been creeping upwards. Between 2000 and 2018, the number of children aged 0 to 9 years

A senior Slovak couple takes a run in the countryside.

decreased by 8 percent; the number of young people aged 10 to 19 years decreased by 36 percent, and the number of young people aged 20 to 29 years decreased by 25 percent. The increase in average age was partly due to a declining birthrate, as well as an increasing life expectancy. In 2020, the average age of the Slovak population was 41.8 years, which ranked it as number 41 out of 228 countries, in which the country ranked number 1 (in this case, the tiny principality of Monaco) had the oldest population, with an average age of 55.4 years, and number 228, Niger, had the youngest, with an average age of 14.8.

In 2020, the country as a whole experienced a negative population growth rate of −0.05 percent, which means the population figures are dropping. Factors that affect this are a falling birthrate (number of births per year per 1,000 population) and a corresponding falling fertility rate (average number of births per woman); immigration/emigration rates; and life expectancy rate.

Girls in colorful, embroidered Slovak costumes celebrate the Easter holiday with baskets full of eggs and flowers.

MINORITY REPORT

The European Union (EU) initially denied membership to Slovakia. Bigotry directed against ethnic minorities, specifically Hungarians and Roma, was cited.

Historians believe the Roma migrated from the Punjabi region of northwestern India to Central and Eastern Europe in the 14th century. Today, they live throughout Europe, and in fact, throughout the world. In Slovakia, they are mostly concentrated in the eastern part of the country. Their traditions, culture, language, and way of life effectively isolate their communities from their neighbors. This isolation is one of the causes of widespread prejudice against them.

Prejudice against Roma people is common throughout Europe. Negative attitudes toward the ethnic group are deep-rooted. In 2019, a Pew Research poll found that 76 percent of Slovaks held unfavorable views of the Roma. Roma communities tend to live on the margins of society, in deep poverty, huddled in slums. Men claim they cannot find work because of bias, and the

Young people gather in a Roma settlement on the outskirts of Janovce, Slovakia.

Slovak opinion polls rate the armed forces as the most respected national institution. Slovakia's governments, often shaky coalitions, may come and go, but the military is a stable establishment and commands the respect of the citizenry.

Slovakia's armed forces consist of the army, the air force, and special operations forces. Since Slovakia is a landlocked country, there is no navy. These units participate in NATO and UN operations.

In 2006, the military became all voluntary, and compulsory service in peacetime was ended. Service is open to people ages 18 to 30, and women are eligible to join. In 2016, the number of active personnel was about 17,000 soldiers and 4,800 civilians.

Spectators watch the Slovak National Uprising Anniversary military parade on August 29, 2019, in Banska Bystrica.

unemployment rate among them is extremely high (reliable statistics are unavailable). Those who can find work often find it in the black market or in occasional day labor that falls outside the mainstream economy. Some support their families on government welfare, causing angry Slovaks to accuse the Roma of being lazy and blithely living off the taxpayers.

According to the European Roma Rights Centre (ERRC), Roma people in Slovakia endure racism at every level of society—in the job market, housing, and education. They are often subjected to forced evictions, hate crimes and vigilante intimidation, and disproportionate levels of police brutality.

In schools, the educational achievement of Roma children falls far below that of other Slovak children. Roma children are often segregated in their own classrooms, or even into their own schools. A 2016 study by the EU's Agency for Fundamental Rights found that 62 percent of Roma children in Slovakia were educated in segregated classrooms or schools—more than in any

Roma children hang out on the stairs of a segregated housing project on the outskirts of Kosice in the eastern part of Slovakia.

other European country. This was despite a 2012 court decision that banned separating students by ethnicity.

The government has worked to improve conditions for the Roma. Housing programs are underway. There is a major effort to reduce the number of Roma afflicted with tuberculosis. There are retraining programs to deal with high Roma unemployment. Most importantly, there are preschool and early-childhood programs to help Roma children who may have grown up speaking their own language rather than Slovak. Nevertheless, the problem of discrimination and prejudice against Roma in Slovakia is far from solved.

INTERNET LINKS

https://www.aljazeera.com/indepth/features/2017/04/life -slovakia-roma-slums-poverty-segregation-170425090756677.html
This in-depth article details the desperate lives endured by Roma people in Slovakia.

https://www.cia.gov/library/publications/the-world-factbook/geos/ lo.html
The *CIA World Factbook* provides demographic data for Slovakia.

http://www.errc.org
The European Roma Rights Centre has a wealth of articles about the Roma in Slovakia.

LIFESTYLE

A Slovak father and daughter enjoy some time together at a mountain lake.

7

I N GENERAL, LIFE IN SLOVAKIA IS GOOD and getting better. Compared to life in some wealthier nations, it may be a simpler life, less cluttered with stuff, but a good one.

Of course, this is a generalization; Slovakia certainly has its problems. The dramatic economic and political reforms that have swept the country since 1993, when independence was declared, have led to many social transformations, and transition can be hard. As Slovakia moved from communism to capitalism, influences from the West impacted upon traditional culture in a variety of ways, for better and for worse.

Recent surveys show that Slovaks' general life satisfaction rating is slightly below the EU average, but rising. The World Health Organization's WHO-5 Well-Being Index, which measures mental well-being, showed improvement for Slovaks from 59 points in 2011 to 67 points in 2016, putting them above the EU average of 64 that year.

RURAL AND URBAN LIFESTYLES

Many Slovak families have lived for generations in small rural villages located in the midst of agricultural areas. Essentially conservative and bound by cultural traditions, the people here have had difficulty coping with changes brought about by the transition to a free-market economy in an independent Slovakia.

The living standard of farmers and agricultural workers has decreased dramatically. When state farms and farm cooperatives were abolished

In 2019, the Global Peace Index found Slovakia to be the 23rd most peaceful of 163 nations. In a "state of peace" range from "very high" to "very low," Slovakia's score placed it in the "high" category. The Czech Republic scored even higher, at number 10, in the "very high" state of peace category. That year, Iceland was number 1, and Afghanistan was last, at number 163. For comparison, that year, the United States received a "low" rank of 128th.

A small village is nestled in the valleys of the Velka Fatra Mountains of northwestern Slovakia.

after communism, many families were plunged into debt. Poorly educated and unskilled except in farmwork, rural Slovaks had a very difficult time making ends meet. For example, the Banska Bystrica region in the south-central area of the country, which is covered with forests and agricultural lands, experienced a very high level of unemployment.

THE LURE OF THE CITY Because of the lack of opportunity, young people in the rural areas have left in search of work. Many have permanently relocated to larger towns, where there is some industry, or moved to the Czech Republic. This has left many parts of rural Slovakia with an aging, impoverished population. In areas where the Roma live, the poverty is even more acute.

In urban centers, however, where younger people predominate, there is greater optimism about the future. For the most part, membership in the European Union has been a step toward greater prosperity.

A COSMOPOLITAN GENERATION

In Bratislava, where the population is growing daily, the city is packed with members of Slovakia's now westernized generation. A great deal of private investment has gone into renovating the capital city to attract tourism. Bratislava is booming, with new restaurants, a thriving café and bar scene, and an energetic cultural life. Kosice, the second-largest city, also has a lively cosmopolitan atmosphere and a newly rejuvenated town square. There is significant industry in the area, which attracts Slovaks looking for a good place to live and work.

Slovaks are quickly increasing their connections to the international community as the government funds improvements to the country's communications systems, including additional phone lines, fiber-optic cable, and digital equipment. The country has a modern telecommunications system, with rapid growth in broadband, including wireless options. Slovakia has 2 public and around 50 private television stations, and 32 privately owned radio stations.

People enjoy a warm day on the streets of the Old Town section of Bratislava.

About 40 percent of households are connected to cable or satellite TV. Around 80 percent of Slovaks have access to the internet, and virtually everyone has a cell phone. Facebook is the most popular social network, followed by the domestic platform Pokec.sk.

WOMEN AND FAMILIES

Slovakia tends to hold conservative social values, and traditionally, women were expected to stay at home and care for the home and family. To some extent, these attitudes continue to prevail.

In fact, one telling controversy in 2020 was the Slovak government's refusal of the Istanbul Convention. Officially known as the Council of Europe Convention on Preventing and Combating Violence Against Women and Domestic Violence, it is a European initiative aimed at combating violence against women. It characterizes violence against women as a violation of human rights and a form of discrimination. The provision created a legal framework for approaching

A mother and her children pose before Strbske Pleso, the second-largest glacial lake in the Slovak High Tatras.

violence against women, including domestic violence and gender-based violence, which would be consistent across borders.

First adopted in 2011 by the Council of Europe, it had by 2019 acquired the signatures of 46 countries and the EU, including that of Slovakia. However, Slovakia then reversed course and announced it would pull out of the agreement. Certain conservative groups had charged that the convention would lead to an acceptance of same-sex marriage and gender fluidity. Opponents inaccurately accused the convention of having a hidden liberal agenda. Therefore, based on the Slovak government's (and the constitution's) opposition to same-sex marriage, Slovakia refused to ratify the convention.

A cashier rings up a woman's groceries at a supermarket in Kosice.

Meanwhile, nearly one-quarter of Slovak women (23 percent) reported that they had experienced some form of violence from an intimate partner. In addition, an opinion poll carried out in 2016 showed that as many as 40 percent of Slovak respondents believed that rape could be justified in some circumstances.

GENDER EQUITY   When Slovakia joined the EU in 2004, it had one of the widest gender pay gaps in the entire EU community. (A gender pay gap, or wage gap, is the difference between the amounts of money paid to women and men who do the same or similar work. Typically, men are paid more than women for the same work.) That year, Slovakia's parliament adopted the Anti-Discrimination Act, prohibiting discrimination on grounds of sex and gender. In addition, Slovakia's labor code states that women have the right to equal treatment in matters of employment, such as salary, promotion, and training, and that work conditions and arrangements should reflect the family obligations of both women and men.

Things have since improved, but gender equity has not yet been achieved. In 2018, the difference between hourly wages earned by men and women in Slovakia was 19 percent, three points higher than the EU average but lower than Britain (21 percent) and Germany (22 percent). That means that women earned, on average, 81 percent of men's salaries for the same work.

Women make up about 46 percent of the Slovak labor force. The percentage of women with full secondary or university education is slightly higher than that of men, but women earn less in each job category. Women are drawn to fields like education, catering, health care, social work, banking, and insurance, where they encounter a so-called glass ceiling that limits their ability to rise to the highest executive positions. Because of family and childcare duties, women are regarded as undependable and are the first to be fired when there are layoffs. The gender income gap increases between men and women as they grow older.

PARENTAL BENEFITS   Parental leave has replaced maternal leave in the labor code, with benefits distributed accordingly. Now, every employee, woman or man, is entitled to take leave when her or his baby is born. An employer must provide either a mother or a father with up to three years of leave for child rearing. During the first 28 weeks, the employee, woman or man, must be paid 90 percent of her or his salary. After that, they are entitled to a flat-rate monthly allowance. There are extra benefits for single or divorced mothers. Slovakia has one of the most liberal parental-leave programs in Europe.

In addition to time off to care for the infant, the government also provides a one-time birth allowance to cover expenditures related to the needs of the newborn. In 2020, that amount was about $900 for first-, second-, and third-born children. (Subsequent infants in the family receive less.) After that, the government provides a child allowance stipend for parents. In terms of the number of beneficiaries and the amount of funds paid, child allowance is the most extensive state social support benefit offered by the Slovak Republic. The state provides a flat-rate child allowance per month for each dependent child aged up to 25 years, regardless of parental income. In 2020, this amount was about $27 per month, with double that amount for children under the age of 6. The state provides additional childcare benefits as well.

THE FUTURE OF THE FAMILY

The concept of the family unit endures as a highly valued way of life. Slovaks still deeply believe that home and children are the paths to fulfillment and greater happiness. Most Slovaks—around two-thirds in 2016—report a manageable work-life balance that gives them sufficient time and energy to fulfill their family responsibilities.

This devotion is symbolized by the way modern Slovaks continue to cling to customs that have always played a role at wedding celebrations. Treasured family wedding rings are still passed down to new brides through the generations. Parents continue the custom of walking brides and grooms down the aisle. At many weddings, the bride wears a *kroj* (KRAH-yuh), a folk dress highly decorated with sequins that is said to protect the newlyweds from evil spirits. However, the typical Western white wedding dress is also popular.

INTERNET LINKS

https://www.employment.gov.sk/files/slovensky/ministerstvo/analyticke-centrum/english-version_kvalita-tlac.pdf
The Ministry of Labor, Social Affairs and Family offers a report on the population's social well-being in 2014.

https://www.europarl.europa.eu/RegData/etudes/STUD/2017/583140/IPOL_STU(2017)583140_EN.pdf
This 2017 report by the European Parliament examines gender equality in Slovakia.

RELIGION

The Church of Saint Elizabeth, commonly known as the Blue Church, is a Catholic church in Bratislava.

8

S LOVAKIA IS A PREDOMINANTLY
Christian nation, and quite a religious
one at that—at least compared to
its former other half, the Czech Republic
(Czechia), and compared to much of
Western Europe as well, which has become
quite secular in recent years. About
63 percent of Slovaks embrace the Roman
Catholic faith, and another 12 percent are
Protestant or Greek Catholic.
Thirty-one percent say they pray daily.
In neighboring Czechia, only 21 percent
of people are Catholic, while 72 percent
are unaffiliated with any religion. Only
9 percent of Czechs say they pray daily.

After 40 years under Communist Party rule, Slovaks shucked off
the antireligious teachings of the Soviet satellite government and found
their way back to the faith of the ninth-century Christian missionaries
Cyril and Methodius.

The anti-Catholicism nature of the Communist Party government
began in 1948. Besides actively persecuting the Catholic Church and its
clergy, the government revived the traditional antagonism between

While 69 percent
of Slovaks say they
believe in God,
only 29 percent of
people in the Czech
Republic do.

Medieval frescoes cover the interior of the Church of Saint Francis of Assisi in Poniky, Slovakia. The small Roman Catholic church dates from 1310.

Czechs and Slovaks. Slovakia was a more rural, conservative, and religious region than the Czech part of the country. This is still true today.

Following World War II, the Czechoslovakian Communist Party flourished in Prague. It followed that when the Communists came to power, government authority over Slovakia was transferred from Bratislava to Prague. In 1960, a new version of the constitution deprived Slovakia of its right to rule itself and placed Prague firmly in control of the region. Anti-Slovak prejudice and anti-Catholicism were merged in policies that were both ethnically and religiously biased.

COMMUNIST RULE

Under communism, atheism was the only permissible moral doctrine for the Slovak people. Catholicism, which had long been the major Slovak religion, was considered an enemy of the state and the chief target of the Communist Party government. The aim was to wipe out the Catholic Church throughout Czechoslovakia. The result was far more successful in the non-Slovak part of the country.

However, two generations of Slovak children would be indoctrinated with antireligious, anti-Catholic, anti-God beliefs. More than a decade after the collapse of communism in Czechoslovakia, a significant share of the Slovak population still defined themselves as nonbelievers.

On the night of April 13, 1950, with Action K, the Communist Party's designation for the program to dismantle the Catholic Church in Czechoslovakia, all 216 Catholic monasteries in the country were closed. Around 2,400 monks from 28 orders were imprisoned in concentration cloisters. The following autumn, 12,299 Roman Catholic nuns were rounded up, and their 339 convents were taken over for use either by the army or by government institutions.

Action K included the seizing of Roman Catholic seminaries and other church property, the suppression of church publications, police disruption of

The Red Monastery (Cerveny Klastor) is in the Pieniny Mountains of northern Slovakia. The monastery, no longer in use, dates to the early 1300s.

BASIC TENETS OF ROMAN CATHOLICISM

Catholics are, first and foremost, Christians. Like all Christians, they believe in one God, and that Jesus Christ, who was resurrected from the dead, is the Son of God. They believe that the Bible is the Word of God. However, there are essential beliefs and practices that are particular to the Catholic Church. They include:

THE HOLY TRINITY *Catholics believe that God is one, but exists in three persons— God the Father, God the Son, and God the Holy Spirit.*

THE IMMORTAL SOUL *People are made up of a mortal body and an immortal soul, which is the "spiritual principle" in humans. Both the body and soul are created by God, and together they form one unique human nature.*

ORIGINAL SIN *Catholics believe that all people are born with original sin on their soul, passed on to them by the disobedience of Adam and Eve in the biblical Garden of Eden. That sin can be removed only by the sacrament of Baptism, which leaves the soul in a state of grace.*

HOLY SACRAMENTS *Baptism is the first of seven sacraments recognized by the Roman Catholic Church. Sacraments are rites that serve as channels for God's grace. The seven sacraments are: Baptism, Confession (Penance), Communion (the Eucharist), Confirmation, Anointing of the Sick (Extreme Unction), Marriage, and Holy Orders.*

AFTERLIFE *Roman Catholics believe that the soul is immortal, and that after the body dies, the soul is judged. Those that are free of sin enter Heaven, where they exist in the purity and joy of God's grace for eternity. Some souls must first pass through Purgatory to be cleansed of sin before they can enter Heaven. Those who are beyond redemption spend eternity in Hell, blocked forever from God's grace.*

APOSTOLIC SUCCESSION *Roman Catholics believe that the pope is a direct successor of Saint Peter, one of Jesus Christ's 12 Apostles and the first leader of the Catholic Church. As such, the pope is infallible on matters of faith and morals. (However, not everything the pope says, or that the Catholic Church teaches, is held to be infallible. The doctrine of papal and church infallibility is subject to specific conditions.)*

church services, and the arrest of most Slovak bishops, several of whom died in prison.

OTHER RELIGIONS

Roman Catholicism is the foremost religion in Slovakia. It is not, however, the only religion. The second largest group is the atheists, who make up roughly 13 percent of the population. About 8 percent are Protestant.

The estimated Jewish population of Slovakia is thought to be about 2,600. The majority of them live in Bratislava, and there are smaller Jewish communities in Kosice, Presov, Piestany, and Nove Zamky. Most of the historic Slovak Jewish population was wiped out during the Holocaust. Slovakia actively assisted the Nazis in the deportation of around 75,000 Slovak Jews to extermination camps.

There are several small pockets of other religions practiced in Slovakia. These include the Church of Jesus Christ of Latter-Day Saints (Mormons), the

The Jewish synagogue in Trencin is now a cultural center.

THE WOODEN CHURCHES

Slovakia has more than 50 historic wooden churches—the highest density in Europe. Indeed, the "Wooden Churches of the Slovak Part of the Carpathian Mountain Area" is a UNESCO World Heritage listing. The listing consists of eight churches: two Roman Catholic, three Protestant, and three Greek Orthodox churches, all built between the 16th and 18th centuries. Most of them are in isolated villages. All of the wooden churches exhibit the folk architecture of the time, though they present several different styles, reflecting Gothic, Renaissance, and Baroque influences. Inside, they are richly decorated with wall and ceiling paintings.

The wooden church in Hronsek, Slovakia, is one of the churches included in the World Heritage listing.

Brethren Church, Zen Buddhism, and the Baha'i faith. Slovakia has a small Muslim population of less than 0.5 percent. It is estimated that there are only 5,000 Muslims in the country, and most of them live in the capital, Bratislava. Most Muslims are also not native Slovaks—many are refugees, migrant workers, or students. There are very few Muslim communities outside Bratislava.

RELIGION AND THE STATE

The constitution of Slovakia guarantees freedom of religious belief and affiliation, as well as the right to have no religious faith or affiliation. There is no official state religion, and religious groups are protected from government interference in their affairs. However, the constitution does stipulate an exception when "necessary in a democratic society for the protection of public order, health, and morals or for the protection of the rights and freedoms of others."

The 14th-century Basilica of Saint James sits in the main square in Levoca, shown here behind the Old Town Hall. The church is part of the same UNESCO World Heritage site that includes Spis Castle, which is located in the same vicinity.

The Roman Catholic Church of Mary Help of Christians in Bratislava, consecrated in 1990, is an example of modern church architecture.

Churches and other religious groups must register with the government in order to be officially recognized. According to a 2017 legislative amendment, such groups must have a minimum number of 50,000 members (up from the previous 20,000). Unofficial groups may not establish religious schools or receive government funding. Their clergy cannot perform certain functions, such as officiating at weddings or funerals. Critics of the new law charged that it was aimed at preventing the recognition of Islamic groups.

Under the current system, the government pays the wages of clergy members of officially registered and recognized churches and other religious bodies. Some see that as discriminatory against other groups, including non-religious civic organizations. True separation of church and state would mean no governmental financing of churches.

In recent years, state expenditures for registered churches more than doubled. While the state has tried not to interfere in various churches' internal affairs and therefore compromise religious freedom, it has decided to reconsider church financing and tax exemptions. Changing the system of direct state financing of churches and religious societies is currently one of the most widely discussed issues concerning state-church relations in Slovakia.

INTERNET LINKS

https://www.expatfocus.com/slovakia/living/a-brief-guide-to-the -main-religious-beliefs-in-slovakia-2277
A brief overview of religions in Slovakia is provided on this site.

https://www.independent.co.uk/news/world/europe/slovakia-bars -islam-state-religion-tightening-church-laws-robert-fico-a7449646.html
This article alleges the 2017 law requiring registered religions to have 50,000 followers was aimed at preventing Islam from gaining ground in Slovakia.

https://www.pewresearch.org/fact-tank/2019/01/02/once-the -same-nation-the-czech-republic-and-slovakia-look-very-different -religiously
This article examines the different attitudes toward religion in Czechia and Slovakia.

https://slovakia.travel/en/things-to-see-and-do/culture-and -sights/wooden-churches
Some of the most notable wooden churches in Slovakia are pictured and described on this travel site.

http://www.slovak-republic.org/religion/churches
This site lists Slovakia's notable churches, cathedrals, and other religious buildings.

https://whc.unesco.org/en/list/1273
This is the page for the Wooden Churches in Slovakia UNESCO World Heritage site.

LANGUAGE

A book store offers its wares in the historic Old Town section of Banska Stiavnica.

9

SLOVAK IS THE OFFICIAL LANGUAGE of Slovakia. It is one of the West Slavic subdivisions of Slavic languages derived from the Indo-European language grouping. Other West Slavic languages include Czech, Polish, Upper Sorbian, and Lower Sorbian. Slovak is very closely related to Czech, and to a large extent, the two languages are mutually intelligible. Spoken by most of Slovakia's 5.4 million people, Slovak is easily understood by other Slavs as well.

A VOICE FOR THE PEOPLE

Language was key to the independence movements of the peoples ruled by the Hungarian Empire, including the Slovaks, during the 19th century. The Magyars (ethnic Hungarians), although only about 4 percent of the total population of the Hungarian confederation, insisted on the Magyarization of the country as a whole. This meant that Magyar culture became the established culture. Magyar lords owned most of the estates, while non-Magyar populations were mostly relegated to serfdom. The Magyar language was the language of the land.

Slovak is one of the 23 official languages of the European Union. There are fewer official languages than members states because some of the languages are spoken in several countries. However, most EU business is conducted in English, French, and German. Documents are translated into the other languages as needed by the members of the European Parliament.

a . . . sounds like u *in but*
á . . . like a *in father*
ä . . . like e *in pet*
b . . . like b *in boy*
c . . . like ts *in bits*
č . . . like ch *in child*
ch . . . like ch *in Loch Ness*
d . . . like d *in dog*
d' . . . like the dy *sound in dew*
dz . . . like zz *in pizza*
dž . . . like j *in jug*
e . . . like e *in set*
é . . . like ai *in pair*
f . . . like f *in fan*
g . . . like g *in go*
h . . . like h *in hat*
i . . . like i *in sit*
í . . . like ee *in cheese*
j . . . like y *in yes*
k . . . like k *in kernel*
l . . . like l *in last*
ĺ . . . approximately like lll *(a "long l")*
l' . . . approximately like lyuh
m . . . like m *in mat*

n . . . like n *in now*
ň . . . like gn *in lasagna*
o . . . like o *in odd*
ó . . . like aw *in saw*
ô . . . like wo *in wonder*
p . . . like p *in pool*
q . . . like kv
r . . . like a rolled r
s . . . like s *in save*
š . . . like sh *in she*
t . . . like t *in top*
t' . . . approximately like tyuh
u . . . like u *in put*
ú . . . like oo *in choose*
v . . . like v *in very; or like* w *in wind if before a consonant or at the end of a word*
w . . . like Slovak v
x . . . like x *in fox*
y . . . like i *in sit*
ý . . . like ee *in cheese*
z . . . like z *in zone*
ž . . . like s *in pleasure*

The empire's other groups, including the Slovaks, rebelled against this and, as a matter of ethnic pride, stubbornly persisted in using their own languages. However, these languages were not, for the most part, organized systematically, nor were they arranged according to strict grammatical rules. These languages, both in their spoken and written forms, were subject to local interpretations. Intellectuals who also considered themselves ethnic patriots were frustrated and came to consider language as the most important part of establishing and preserving their culture.

The formulation of a Slovak language was to become the life's work of Ludovit Stur. Stur was born on October 28, 1815, in the Slovak village of Zay-Uhrovec (now Uhrovec). Stur was baptized in the Evangelical Lutheran Church and received his basic education from his schoolteacher father. This included a thorough grounding in Latin that was the basis for his career in linguistics.

In 1827, Stur was sent to Gyor in present-day Hungary, where he became interested in history and proficient in Hungarian, German, and Greek. He continued his language studies at the Evangelical Lutheran Lyceum in Bratislava and eventually joined the Czech-Slav Society, which by the early 1830s was concerning itself with both language and politics.

To support himself, Stur gave private lessons at the lyceum, which was connected with the Czech-Slav Society. He established important contacts with foreign and Czech scholars, and in 1834, he was elected secretary of the society. By 1835, he had become co-editor of the society's magazine, *Plody* ("Fruits"), which published several of his poems. In 1836, Stur wrote a letter to the leading Czech historian, Frantisek Palacky, pointing out that the Czech language had evolved into an incomprehensible tongue for Slovaks—particularly Protestant Slovaks.

A statue of Ludovit Stur stands in the main square in Levoca.

A BATTLEGROUND OF WORDS

Stur proposed the creation of a merged Czecho-Slovak language in which Czechs would use some Slovak words and Slovaks would adopt some Czech phrases. The Czechs absolutely rejected such a compromise. By now, Stur had acquired a following among Slovaks. It was decided to shelve any idea of merging the Czech and Slovak languages and to create a new Slovak language instead. The West Slovak language, derived from the Indo-European language grouping, would be the basis of the movement.

The subkingdoms of the Hungarian Empire were in rebellion against the Magyarization of their various cultures. Respective national independence crusades were an integral part of the different language movements. The situation grew even more complicated when, in 1848, the Hungarian revolution against Austrian rule, based in Vienna, combined the struggle to free the peasants from serfdom with attempts to establish a variety of independence movements with nationalistic claims.

The Slovak nationalists were part of the anti-Austrian forces during the Hungarian revolution and were opposed to the Magyarization the Hungarians wished to establish once they were out from under the Austrian yoke. Stur and other Slovak patriots were carrying on a campaign to establish a strictly Slovak culture on the bedrock of a newly created Slovak language.

As pride in Slovak culture took hold, there arose opposition to merging it with any other culture, particularly Czech. In May 1848, a huge public meeting was held in Liptovsky Mikulas, where an ethnic Slovak program known as the Requirements of the Slovak Nation was proclaimed. It was widely accepted by the Slovak people.

This manifesto was backed by force of Slovak arms against the Austrians, the Magyars, the Czechs, and others. While Stur and his supporters were creating a purely Slovak language, which gained surprisingly wide acceptance among the Slovak people, a Slovak-run government was formed.

It did not last long. Politics prevailed. In 1849, the Russians became involved and helped the Austrians defeat the Magyar revolutionaries. In 1851, the Austrian emperor Franz Joseph abolished constitutional rule in Slovakia and imposed himself as absolute ruler. The crusade for Slovak nationalism had been crushed but not eradicated. The Slovak language created by Stur and his followers prevailed.

Efforts to stamp out the new language scored temporary successes, but there was a lack of either will or coordination to halt publication of works in Slovak written by Stur and others. There were efforts to stop the teaching of Slovak in schools, but since most Slovaks spoke and understood it, the language prevailed. Today, Slovak is the language standard used throughout Slovakia

and among Slovaks elsewhere. It is an accepted fact that Stur's battle for a Slovak language has been won.

Stur paid a price for his victory. He was not permitted to publish a newspaper in the Slovak language. He lived in the suburb of Modra (near Bratislava) under close police supervision from 1851 until his death in January 1856. Many of his poems are still in print, and Slovak schoolchildren memorize them. They celebrate Slovak nationhood, and they do so in the Slovak language that Stur created.

DIALECTS

There are three major dialects in the Slovak language: Central Slovak, Western Slovak, and Eastern Slovak. Central Slovak forms the basis of the standard language.

Groups separated by Slovakia's numerous mountain ranges have developed regionally distinctive slangs, word-shortenings, and pronunciations. For the most part, these dialects are mutually understood, much like those in the United States—New Englanders and Floridians understand each other, as do New Yorkers and Californians.

Some of the dialects fade into a border-region terminology common to neighboring nations. Thus, some Slovak frontier dialects merge with Czech, Ruthenian, or Polish dialects, affecting both vocabulary and pronunciation.

Written in the Roman, or Latin, alphabet, Slovak employs several special accents that can change the pronunciation of a specific letter. A modified Roman system of spelling has been adopted. Like other Slavic languages, Slovak has a complicated grammar. For instance, nouns are feminine, masculine, or neuter, and a noun may have one of six declensions (endings) to express gender, number, person, and case, or combinations of these.

Slovakia's National Radio Headquarters in Bratislava is shaped like an upside-down pyramid. The radio network broadcasts in Slovak and in Hungarian, the largest minority language.

A system of defining old information versus new information is peculiar to arranging sequences and defining emphasis in the Slovak language. Phrases containing old information precede those with new information or those that are meant to have more emphasis. Slovak has six short vowel phonemes (groupings of closely related speech sounds), one of which is hardly ever used. There are also five long vowel sounds and four diphthongs, which are combinations of multiple vowel sounds. Consonants at the ends of words are often silent.

OTHER LANGUAGES

While Slovak is the native tongue of 78.6 percent of Slovakia's residents, there are a number of ethnic minorities living in the country who speak other languages, including Hungarian, Romani, Czech, Moravian, Silesian, Ruthenian, Ukrainian, German, and Polish.

Hungarians are the largest minority, concentrated largely in the southern part of the country and making up about 20 percent of the regional population. About 8.5 percent of Slovaks speak Hungarian.

The large Roma community lives mostly in the east and speaks five dialects of the Carpathian Romani and Vlax Romani languages.

Czechs, Germans, and Poles live throughout the country, while Ruthenians live primarily in the east and northeast.

INTERNET LINKS

https://www.omniglot.com/writing/slovak.htm
This language site presents an introduction to Slovak.

https://www.slovakia.com/facts/slovak-language
Sample phrases and pronunciations are offered on this page.

ARTS

A street artist makes bubbles for children outside the old Slovak National Theatre in Old Town, Bratislava.

A COUNTRY'S ARTS REFLECT ITS history, culture, and the overall life of its people. Nationhood and ethnic identity have been the key influences on the arts in Slovakia throughout its history, including its roles as part of the Austro-Hungarian Empire and subsequently of Czechoslovakia, its short existence as a Nazi satellite, its subjugation under communism, and its present status as an independent state. Each of these periods left its mark on the various arts of Slovakia. Each has been incorporated into the strong ethnic identity of those arts.

LITERATURE

There can be no denying the strong influence of Austro-Hungarian sentimentality on Slovak literature. The so-called Stur period of Slovak fiction and poetry that followed the death of Ludovit Stur in 1856 borrowed noticeably from the romantic style of Austro-Hungarian writers. At the same time, there was a marked folk flavor to Slovak works that glorified the culture of the Slovak people.

A subtle Slovak humor marked works such as the stylish romantic poem *Marina*, by Andrej Sladkovic. Sometimes called "the world's longest love poem," the national epic has 291 stanzas and 2,900 lines. Slovak comedies were distinguished from the light, frivolous Austro-Hungarian works by the point of view of a minor character commenting with sly cultural overtones on the plot from a dry, tongue-in-cheek, lower-class Slovak perspective.

Sometimes, however, ethnic pride went too far for the Austro-Hungarians. Janko Kral, whose epics and poems were the most outspoken examples of Slavic romanticism, and who narrowly escaped execution during the 1848 revolution, was a thorn in the side of the government until his death in 1876. Today, Kral is a major literary hero of Slovakia.

Poetry and drama were important factors in establishing Slovak culture under Austro-Hungarian rule. Dramatists like Jan Chalupka and Jan Palarik wrote popular comedies that tweaked the sensibilities of the ruling establishment and their views of class, culture, and ethnic superiority. At the turn of the 20th century, the poetry of Pavol Orszagh Hviezdoslav introduced the literature

A statue of the writer Janko Kral adorns a park in Bratislava.

Just as UNESCO (the United Nations Educational, Scientific and Cultural Organization) works to protect natural and cultural World Heritage sites, it also identifies examples of "Intangible Cultural Heritage of Humanity" that need to be preserved. These include, according to the group's website, "traditions or living expressions inherited from our ancestors and passed on to our descendants, such as oral traditions, performing arts, social practices, rituals, arts, festive events, knowledge and practices concerning nature and the universe or the knowledge and skills to produce traditional crafts."

The Convention for the Safeguarding of the Intangible Cultural Heritage has listed seven entries for Slovakia. These are drotarstvo, *a wire craft and art;* modrotlac, *a block printing method using indigo dye; the multipart singing of Horehronie; puppetry in Slovakia and Czechia; bagpipe culture; the music of Terchova; and the* fujara *(a type of flute, pronounced FOO-yuh-ruh) and its music.*

A traditional craftsperson weaves a bowl from wire.

and pride of the Slovak people to the outside world. His work continues to be widely translated today.

After World War II, Communist Party ideology was heavily imposed on Slovak literature. The most famous Slovak work of the period was *Kronika* ("Chronicle") by Peter Jilemnicky. *Kronika* is a brilliant and massive work filled with anticapitalist themes and heroic workers. The lower-class Slovak hero continued to be a favorite character after the fall of communism. Today, Slovaks continue to take pride in books featuring folk wisdom and village heroes like those in the stories of Bozena Slancikova, who was better known by her pen name, Timrava.

Few contemporary Slovak writers are known by or published in the English-speaking world, but that doesn't mean they don't exist.

MUSIC

Slovakia has a rich heritage of folk music that began hundreds of years ago, when singers of heroic tales traveled from village to village to entertain the

Traditionally dressed musicians perform at a folk music and dance festival in the town of Cerveny Klastor.

people. These melodies were passed down through the centuries. German and Hungarian immigrants also contributed their music to this folk tradition.

In the 19th century, classical composers began using elements of folk music in their compositions. When modern musicologists began to collect examples of folk music, they discovered that a rural style was common in the north and west and included bandit and shepherd songs. In the agricultural plains and valleys, wedding and harvest songs proliferated among the inhabitants.

Traditional instruments that folk musicians perform on include the fujara, a 6-foot-long (1.8 m) flute; the *fanforka* (FUN-fahr-kuh), a reed instrument resembling the clarinet; and bagpipes, called *dudy* (DOO-dih) or *gajdy* (GUHY-dih).

A young man dressed in a Slovak folk costume plays the fujara at a festival.

PAINTING

Prior to Slovakia's independence, the major influences on Slovak painting and sculpture were Hungarian and Bohemian artists, as well as the communist

The Main Altar of Saint Elizabeth at the Cathedral of Saint Elizabeth in Kosice features 12 Gothic paintings dating to the 1470s. They are part of a set of 48 painted scenes. The church itself is the biggest in Slovakia and dates to 1378.

ideology. Elements of all three influences are still visible in works produced by Slovak artists today. However, as they are combined and modernized, a new, uniquely Slovak vision is beginning to appear.

Dating to the 12th century, the earliest Slovak paintings include frescoes by anonymous clerical artists in the churches of Dechtice and Bina. The Spis region offers religious works spanning three centuries and culminating in the 15th-century panels of Levoca's Basilica of Saint James and Kosice's Cathedral of Saint Elizabeth. The old wooden churches of eastern Slovakia offer some of the best Gothic paintings and icons to be found in the former countries of the Austro-Hungarian Empire.

Among the first painters of the Slovak Baroque school to achieve recognition were Jakub Bogdan and Jan Kupecky. They were succeeded by Jan Kracker and Anton Maulbertsch, who produced what are considered to be the most

decorative Baroque works in Slovakia. They may be viewed in the Jasov and the Chapel of the Assumption in Trencianske Bohuslavice.

The flourishing of Hungarian art in the 19th century encouraged the Slovak National Revival, which saw Slovak painters branching out from religious subjects. Among them were Dominik Skutecky, who took as his themes the day-to-day activities of peasants and workers in the Banska Bystrica area. The revival also featured the colorful landscapes of Ladislav Mednansky and the expressive portraits by Peter Bohun.

One of the most important Slovak artists of the 20th century was Ludovit Fulla. His bright, colorful canvases evoke folk art and modernism. Today, a gallery dedicated to his art, which holds 548 of his paintings, drawings, and works of graphic art, attracts visitors to the town of Ruzomberok, where he spent his final years.

Visitors regard a Ludovit Fulla painting in his gallery in Ruzomberok.

SCULPTURE

Sculpture evolved along with painting from the 12th through the 19th centuries. The movable, painted wood figures of the craftsman Pavol of Levoca are superb early examples of Gothic sculpture. Master Stefan of Kosice produced some of the first works in stone. His landmark sculptures can be viewed at the Cathedral of Saint Elizabeth in Kosice.

The leading sculptor of the early 18th-century Baroque era was Georg Raphael Donner, an Austrian who worked in Bratislava. His *Saint Martin and the Beggar* is the showpiece of the Saint Martin Cathedral in Bratislava. Both sculpture and painting in Slovakia enjoyed a rebirth encouraged by the Bohemian art movement that sprang up following the birth of Czechoslovakia after World War I. Portrayals of village life typify the work of artists of the period.

Under communism, the government encouraged Slovak art that celebrated workers and the collective manufacturing process in order to promote the progress of the state. Typical of the style is the Red Army Memorial by

A bronze sculpture, *Bosorka* (*Slovak Witch*) by Tibor Bartfay, is a contemporary piece on the grounds of Bratislava Castle, dedicated to women who were convicted of witchcraft.

sculptor Julius Bartfay, just outside Bratislava.

After independence, many artists reacted against the previous decades. Stano Filko, who had been banned by the government, became prominent with works that juxtaposed and highlighted military weapons and war supplies. A more personal technique by young artists such as Klara Bokayova and Martin Knut marks an increasingly popular modern trend in Slovak art today.

Distinctive folk designs embellish the exterior walls of wooden houses in the Slovak village of Cicmany.

FOLK ARTS AND CRAFTS

Folk arts and crafts developed throughout Slovak history. They flourish today chiefly in the northeastern areas of Spis, Bardejov, Svidnik, and Humenne. Tools, kitchen utensils, musical instruments, and furniture are still made by hand with intricate folk designs.

Traditional folk dress is designed with complicated pictorial or abstract embroidery in gay colors. Fabric weaving, glass painting, and wood carving are popular in rural areas. The folk tradition of painting houses with bright colors can be seen throughout Slovakia. Some of these structures are decorated with carved or molded plaster. These traditional arts and crafts are handed down from one generation to another and are preserved by the government through museum exhibitions.

FILM

Slovak film only emerged after World War II. When the Czech and Slovak republics were united, films were made with combined crews and are referred to today as Czechoslovakian films. In the 1960s, several new-wave directors

made important films that included Jan Kadar and Elmar Klos's *Smrt si rika Engelchen* (*Death Is Called Engelchen*) in 1963. They also directed *Obchod na korze* (*The Shop on Main Street*) in 1965, an Oscar-winning film that dealt with the effects of Nazism. In 1976, Dusan Hanak directed the first Roma feature, which depicted a relationship between a Roma woman and a *gadjo* (GUH-dyah), or non-Roma man.

Under communism, filmmakers suffered from restrictions on their freedom of expression. Although Slovaks continue to make films, filmmakers

Actors Hans Matheson and Anna Friel pose with Slovak writer-director Juraj Jakubisko during the filming of *Bathory*, a 2008 historical drama and Jakubisko's first film shot in English.

are now hampered by reductions in government subsidies. Juraj Jakubisko ranks among the most important Slovak filmmakers since independence. Between 1967 and 2008, he directed 15 feature films, and he has won many international awards.

ARCHITECTURE

The castles of eastern Slovakia are some of the finest and most spectacular examples of fortress architecture in Central and Eastern Europe. Spissky Hrad, also called Spis Castle, dates to 1209 and is a UNESCO World Heritage site. With its jutting parapets and angled battlements set against a craggy mountain sky, it is one of the most photographed structures in Slovakia.

Other castles of importance that have been restored include those at Zvolen and Bratislava. Slovakia's first Christian church was built in Nitra in 833. It no longer exists, but Nitra's Saint Emmeram's Cathedral contains a tiny 11th-century Romanesque chapel that includes remnants of the early church's structure. Dating to 1002, the Romanesque remains of a Benedictine monastery located in Diakovce are thought to be the oldest religious structure still standing in the country.

JURAJ JAKUBISKO

Juraj Jakubisko has been directing films since 1967. He was born in Kojsov and graduated from the Department of Photography at the School of Applied Arts in Bratislava. He studied at the Prague Film Academy (FAMU) and graduated in 1966.

At first, Jakubisko wanted to be a cameraman. Growing up, he had been inspired by the camera work in classic films such as Orson Welles's Citizen Kane *and Sergei Eisenstein's* Battleship Potemkin. *Of the more modern directors, the Italian director Michelangelo Antonioni was his major inspiration. To get into film school, though, for complicated reasons, he needed to apply to become a director, and the die was cast.*

His early films, produced during his time at FAMU, received several awards. Soon after graduation at age 27, he made Christ's Years, *his first feature film, which symbolized a goodbye to youth and its illusions. It was with his second feature,* The Deserter and the Nomads, *that he began his practice of using Slovak folklore, song, and dance to evoke fables of love and death on film. He drew upon his childhood memories of life in the remote village of Kojsov. As with several other films, Jakubisko did his own camera work on* The Deserter and the Nomads. *His next two features established his international reputation.*

While being praised abroad, Jakubisko was prevented from working on original film projects for nearly 10 years by Slovak politics. After the 1968 uprisings, the leader Alexander Dubcek, who had tolerated artistic freedom, was removed from power and replaced by the communist Gustav Husak. He banned Jakubisko's completed films and halted work on See You in Hell, Friends. *During this period, Jakubisko was made to work on several harmless documentary projects to keep him quiet. Eventually, he was permitted to film again, but when he rewrote a script about a positive socialist hero (*Build a House, Plant a Tree*) to present a more complex main character, his film was again banned in his own country.*

*By the end of the 1980s, Jakubisko worked in relative freedom and made a feature that dealt with the Communist Party takeover after World War II (*Sitting on a Branch, Enjoying Myself*). Regarded as the most popular Slovak director of all time, Jakubisko faced controversy when he moved his production company to Prague in the mid-1990s. His reputation was nonetheless ensured when he released his most ambitious film to date,* An Ambiguous Report About the End of the World *(1997). Jakubisko went on to write and direct his first English-language film,* Bathory, *which was released in 2008.*

Straight out of a fairy tale, Bojnice Castle, parts of which date to the 12th century, is managed by the Slovak National Museum. Fittingly, it's the site of the annual International Festival of Ghosts and Spooks each spring.

In small villages that stretch from Svidnik to the Ukrainian border, where the remaining Slavic people who were originally from Ruthenia still live, there are wooden churches representative of folk architecture. These are part of another World Heritage site, the Wooden Churches of the Slovak Part of the Carpathian Mountain Area. Most of the churches were built during the 18th century. Constructed chiefly of spruce, they are located in serene country settings. Metal nails were not used in the construction, because they symbolized Jesus Christ's crucifixion. The churches consist of three parts—the sanctuary, the altar, and the nave, which together represent the Holy Trinity. In each church is an iconostasis, a wall decorated with icons separating the sanctuary and altar from the nave.

Seventeenth-century Slovak aristocrats and wealthy merchants built their homes in the Baroque style. Many of these structures are notable for their elaborate stucco work. This style is represented by the Cathedral of Saint John the Baptist in Trnava. Architectural influences from Budapest and Vienna contributed to several structures erected in the Art Nouveau style in the late

19th and early 20th centuries. An excellent example is the Church of Saint Elizabeth in Bratislava, designed by the Hungarian architect Odon Lechner. Under communism, many monumental structures were built, including the New Bridge in Bratislava.

INTERNET LINKS

https://www.hisour.com/ludovit-fulla-15981
Ludovit Fulla's life and works are presented on this site, along with an audio reading.

https://ich.unesco.org/en/state/slovakia-SK
The Intangible Cultural Heritage website for Slovakia has links to its listed elements.

https://www.sng.sk/en
The Slovak National Gallery site presents information on a range of Slovak fine arts in its exhibitions pages.

https://theculturetrip.com/europe/slovakia/articles/a-weekend-of-music-and-history-in-bratislava-slovakia
This article describes arts and architecture experiences in Bratislava.

https://whc.unesco.org/en/list/620
This the World Heritage listing for Spis Castle and the associated cultural monuments in Levoca.

https://whc.unesco.org/en/list/1273
The listing for the Wooden Churches of the Slovak Part of the Carpathian Mountain Area can be found here.

LEISURE

Children play near the fountain in the Kosice city center.

SLOVAKIA'S MOUNTAINS, RIVERS, and lakes offer many opportunities for outdoor activities. Skiing, hiking, cycling, and water sports are very popular. Serious spelunkers explore the beautiful caves that enhance the countryside. In addition, the large number of mineral springs has led to the establishment of numerous spas and health resorts located near spa towns, which locals and tourists alike visit during their vacations. As in many other European countries, soccer and ice hockey are the most popular spectator sports.

SPELUNKING

A network of over 3,800 caves weaves through Slovakia. The best-known ones have been declared national monuments. Only 12 are currently open to members of the public, who delve into them to see their intriguing formations.

Since 2007, Slovakia's top footballer (soccer player) has been Marek Hamsik. An eight-time Slovak Footballer of the Year award winner, he became the country's top goal scorer in 2019, with 25 career goals for the national team. Another top Slovak athlete is Peter Sagan, a cyclist who rides for UCI WorldTeam Bora-Hansgrohe.

Stalactites hang from the rock surfaces in the Harmanecka Cave in the Kremnica Mountains.

The Demanovska Ice Cave, in the Low Tatras, was first written about in 1719. It is 5,740 feet (1,750 m) long, with ice filling in the bottom. The Harmanecka Cave, situated to the northwest of Banska Bystrica, is home to nine different species of bats. A walk through the cave takes the spelunker through several tiny passages less than 3 feet (0.9 m) wide that open dramatically into enormous, spacious halls. A trip through the cave takes about an hour and a half. This cave has been familiar to locals since ancient times.

SKIING AND SNOWBOARDING

From December through April, fans of snow sports flock to the High and Low Tatras. Some ski areas provide artificial snow at other times of the year. One of the most visited ski centers is Jasna, the largest area devoted to this

sport in the country. Located in Low Tatras National Park, Jasna is situated on the slopes of Chopok Peak. It has been the site of several World Cup ski races. The High Tatras have many ski resorts, as does the Vratna Valley in the Mala Fatra Mountains. Snowboarding has increased in popularity at ski centers, as the resorts have been improving their terrain to accommodate this sport.

Skiers enjoy the snow-covered trails at Strbske Pleso, a winter resort in the High Tatras.

WATER SPORTS

White-water canoeing and kayaking are enjoyed by hardy Slovaks in the spring. It is then that the swift streams created by the melting snows of winter flow down the mountains. Rivers popular for these activities are the upper Vah and the Hron. Located in Pieniny National Park, the Dunajec River forms part

of the border between Slovakia and Poland. It is heavily used by members of both countries for rafting.

Slovakia has produced several world and Olympic champions in water-sport competitions. As of 2020, its athletes have won a total of 28 medals at the Summer Olympic Games, mostly in slalom canoeing. Slovak athletes have also won 8 medals at the Winter Olympic Games.

HIKING AND CYCLING

Slovakia is a prime area for hiking. There is a network of well-marked and connected trails. These extensive color-coded trails are maintained by the Slovak Hiking Club, an organization that provides very useful hiking maps. The practice of marking and keeping up the trails began near the town of Banska Stiavnica in 1874. Recommended trails are of varying lengths and for

different degrees of skill. Some of the best hikes are in the High Tatras, Mala Fatra, Slovak Paradise, and Slovak Karst National Parks. All offer spectacular views of breathtaking scenery.

Many Slovaks are avid cyclists. Mountain bikes are the equipment of choice for this sport, as most trails are very hilly. There is a well-known biking route that links Bratislava with Vienna, Austria.

Hikers climb up a steep meadow in the Mala Fatra Mountains. Velky Rozsutec Peak rises in the background.

SPAS

Hundreds of mineral springs dot the Slovak landscape. Spas that promote health and encourage relaxation are located near these springs. The Roman legions of Emperor Marcus Aurelius, who ruled the Roman Empire from 161 to 180 CE, bathed in the springs when they came through the area that is now Slovakia.

Located northeast of Bratislava, the spa town of Piestany has a long history of treating rheumatic illnesses. Archaeologists date settlers in this area as far back as 80,000 years ago. Celtic, Germanic, and old Slavic civilizations made use of the curative waters. Many prominent medical doctors visited the town, including the personal physicians to three emperors of the Holy Roman Empire. Composer Ludwig van Beethoven was a guest. Napoleon rode his horse into one of the pools, now called the Napoleon Baths.

The treatment for arthritic ailments and for those with recent orthopedic injuries consists of hot springs and mud baths. This regimen is accompanied by exercise and special diets. Years ago, visitors bathed in pits covered with mats or tree branches along the banks of the Vah River. In 1813, lodging was constructed around the springs.

Despite being a major tourist draw, Piestany has resisted commercial development and still offers a soothing, stress-free environment to visitors.

The historic spa town of Piestany still caters to the health and well-being of its visitors.

Thermal springs and mud baths are believed by some to cure and prevent illnesses and to prolong life. Near the springs are large deposits of healing mud and peat, which are applied to the body during spa visits. Many of the waters have been designated for healing specific ailments. Bardejovske Kupele, a spa in Bardejov in eastern Slovakia, is noted for curing stomach problems and respiratory diseases. Piestany, a spa town in western Slovakia, is visited by those seeking treatment for rheumatism and nervous disorders.

INTERNET LINKS

https://www.slovakia.com/sports
A quick overview of Slovak leisure activities is provided on this site.

https://spectator.sme.sk/c/20060073/exploring-slovakias-caverns-and-caves.html
Spelunking in Slovakia's famous caves is the subject of this article.

https://www.statista.com/map/europe/slovakia/sports-recreation
Statistics relating to sports and recreation in Slovakia are listed on this site.

FESTIVALS

A child takes a close look at the Christmas carp that will live in the family bathtub for a day or two before the traditional holiday feast.

B EING A CATHOLIC COUNTRY, Slovakia celebrates the important Christian holidays each year. Easter and Christmas are the most sacred, but there are others as well. The country also observes several patriotic national holidays marking historic events. In late spring through early fall, Slovak cultural traditions are celebrated at folk festivals held in many cities and towns.

PATRIOTIC OBSERVANCES

The year kicks off with Republic Day on January 1. It marks the date in 1993 that the country became an independent nation. Of course, it's also New Year's Day.

Other patriotic holidays throughout the year include May 8, which marks the end of World War II in Europe; August 29, National Uprising Day, which commemorates the time the Slovaks rose up against Nazi Germany in 1944; September 1, Constitution Day; and November 17, Freedom and Democracy Day, which marks the student demonstration against Nazi occupation in 1939, as well as the 1989 demonstrations in Bratislava and Prague that marked the beginning of the Velvet Revolution. There are several other special patriotic and historical days, but they are observed without being official national holidays.

12

The Christmas Eve carp is traditionally purchased alive several days before the holiday. It is kept in the bathtub, theoretically to purify it in clean water and therefore improve its taste. The children of the family typically take great delight in the fish and treat it like a pet right up until the day it's killed and cooked for the holiday feast.

CATHOLIC HOLIDAYS

National holidays of a religious nature include: Epiphany, January 6; Good Friday, Easter Sunday, and Easter Monday (moveable dates); Saints Cyril and Methodius Day, July 5; and Our Lady of Sorrows Day, September 15. Our Lady of the Seven Sorrows, the Virgin Mary, is the patron saint of Slovakia. November 1 is All Saints' Day, and the Christmas holidays span from December 24 to December 26—Christmas Eve, Christmas Day, and Saint Stephen's Day.

CHRISTMAS

The observance of the Christmas season begins on December 6 with Saint Nicholas (Mikulas) Day. Children leave their shoes or boots on the windowsill and in the morning find them filled with goodies. In some areas of Slovakia, this is the traditional day for exchanging gifts, while others wait until Christmas Eve.

During the month of December, preparations for the holiday are ongoing. There are markets set up in every town, with stalls selling handmade pine wreaths, wooden toys, blown-glass ornaments, hand-painted pottery, candles, firecrackers, and original watercolor paintings. Food booths at the markets sell *gulas* (GOO-lush), a stew made from venison, potatoes, and paprika; grilled pork cutlets; and fresh bread spread with lard and dotted with chopped onion. *Slivovica* (SLEE-vah-vee-kuh), or plum brandy, and spiced white wine, both served hot, are traditionally enjoyed with this food.

The highlight of the Christmas celebration takes place on Christmas Eve, called Stedry Den (STEH-dree DEHN), or Generous Day. The week before, Slovaks thoroughly clean their homes and bake an enormous variety of cakes. In the days leading up to Christmas, many people purchase a live carp that is put in the bathtub until the 24th, when the fish is killed and prepared for the evening meal. The tree is also decorated on that day.

Protestant families often go to church in the afternoon, but Catholics attend a two-hour Midnight Mass, which often has standing room only. Groups of young people and children travel from house to house singing carols, and they are given pastries or apples by neighbors. When the food preparations

for the evening meal are completed, many Slovaks walk in large groups to the cemetery to light candles for their loved ones.

Christmas Eve dinner is served at a table decorated with festive candles. A prayer is said, and traditionally the father of the family dips his finger in honey and makes a cross on everyone's forehead. Although the menu differs slightly depending on one's background, there is always carp, cabbage soup, and potato salad. Catholics eat a vegetarian version of the soup on Christmas Eve, while Protestants add smoked meat or sausage. After dinner, gifts are opened next to the tree.

Young Slovak children are taught that baby Jesus brings the presents and angels decorate the tree. On Christmas Day, families celebrate with a big midday

The Christmas market in Bratislava's main square looks magical in the evening light.

meal. Typical foods eaten at Christmas dinner are roast turkey, dumplings, and sauerkraut.

EASTER

The Easter holiday has an unusual combination of sacred and secular traditions. It is the most important religious festival of the year. On Palm Sunday, the week before Easter, it is customary in many villages to adorn a small tree with decorated hollow eggs and ribbons. This tree is carried from house to house by young people who sing blessings for the home and receive eggs in return.

In a tradition still followed in some farming areas, on the Thursday and Friday before Easter, fruit trees are shaken in the belief that this will produce a good crop. Cows are given fresh water so that they will provide more milk, and farmers wash themselves in the cold waters of rivers or creeks to ensure that they will have good health for the next year. In Catholic towns, oil and

A Slovak woman decorates Easter eggs using a traditional wax-resist technique. Here, the candle flame melts the wax off the eggshell to reveal the design.

candle wax are placed in front of the church and set on fire, a blaze called Judas's Fire. This custom is said to ensure a good harvest.

Slovak Christians spend Easter Sunday in church, where they pray to mark the resurrection of Jesus Christ. After church, friends and relatives exchange decorated Easter eggs as gifts. Easter dinner is eaten in the afternoon and consists of ham, lamb, or a kid goat. On Easter Monday, a version of an old custom to keep single women beautiful and healthy is still followed in towns and villages. Males pour or sprinkle water over the women and then beat their legs lightly with a small whip made from a willow called a *korba* (KAHR-buh), while they chant blessings. Afterward, the women give the men chocolates, colored eggs, and schnapps (an alcoholic drink). On the Tuesday after Easter, women pour water over the men who soaked them the day before.

BRATISLAVA MUSIC FESTIVAL

The Bratislava Music Festival, held in autumn for two weeks, has been in existence for more than 50 years. The capital city is an ideal place for this festival, as it has a rich musical tradition—noted classical composers Haydn, Beethoven, and Liszt all performed here. It is an international festival. Musicians from around two dozen countries perform at its concerts. Slovak composers of the past and present are featured. The festival emphasizes the work of talented young artists from many countries who compete for the New Talent of the Year award presented on the second day of the festival.

Although the concerts are mainly chamber and orchestral, other genres, such as jazz, are included. The Slovak Philharmonic performs a work especially commissioned for the festival, and there are several premieres of works written by contemporary Slovak composers. Festival events are promoted by posters designed by Slovak visual artists.

FOLK FESTIVALS

Beginning in late May, cultural festivals are held in dozens of villages, cities, and towns. These festivals celebrate the music, dance, crafts, and traditional dress of the Slovak people.

Folk costumes that are now worn and displayed at festivals were once clothes that people used every day. A more elaborate version was worn on Sundays and holidays and for important events. Although the clothes vary from region to region, the most striking feature is the colorful embroidery hand-stitched on many of the skirts, shirts, aprons, jackets, fur coats, scarves, and pants of both men and women. The traditional linen men's attire was made up of breeches (pants that end at the knee), a shirt with wide sleeves, and an apron. The women wore narrow trousers covered by a shirt without sleeves, a skirt, and an apron. Both men and women sometimes added waistcoats, blazers, belts, overblouses, and fur coats to their outfits. Married women wore a bonnet and a kerchief, while men always wore a hat, which in the colder months was made from fur.

When Slovak folk groups perform a dance at a festival, they wear the costume of the region where the dance originated. Folk songs helped to preserve the Slovak language during the years Slovaks were ruled by other countries. These songs tell of love, mourning, hope for the future, and celebration.

Spectators at the Vychodna Folklore Festival light up a chilly summer evening under the peaks of the High Tatras.

The largest festival in the Tatra Mountains, the three-day Zamagurie Folk Festival, is held in the eastern towns of Spisska Stara Ves and Cerveny Klastor in mid-June. Workshops on traditional dances and crafts demonstrations are given. During the festival, music and dance groups entertain enthusiastic audiences. Included is a performance by a Roma dance ensemble.

For more than 65 years, the Vychodna Folklore Festival, named after a small town in the mountainous Liptov area, has been showcasing Slovak traditions through dances, songs, enactments of customs, and costumes from all over the country. This festival, which takes place over three days in July, has achieved national and international recognition. In addition to participants from Slovakia, the festival hosts folklore performing groups from Georgia, Croatia, Romania, and Hungary.

INTERNET LINKS

https://www.npr.org/sections/thesalt/2014/12/22/372088391/in-slovakia-christmas-dinner-starts-in-the-bathtub
The Slovak tradition of keeping a carp in the bathtub before the Christmas Eve meal is described in this article.

https://www.ricksteves.com/europe/slovakia/festivals
This site lists some of the most notable festivals in Slovakia.

https://www.theguardian.com/world/2015/apr/06/easter-monday-tradition-whipping-slovakia-girls-health
A quick article recounts the tradition of drenching women on Easter Monday.

https://www.timeanddate.com/holidays/slovakia
This calendar site lists Slovak holidays and observances by year.

FOOD

Two men participate in a sausage-making competition at a festival in Litava.

13

SLOVAK CUISINE IS MUCH LIKE THAT of the Czech Republic, which makes sense since the two were once one country. Both food cultures are known for their heavy, meat-based diets, but Slovak cooking tends to show more Hungarian influence, with more spice.

Pork is by far the most popular meat, with ham, sausage, and various pork cuts often found in stews and soups. Beef and chicken are widely favored as well. Dumplings are used more commonly than noodles or potatoes, though potato dumplings, or *halusky*, are a national dish. The small dumplings, similar to gnocchi, are usually topped with *bryndza*, a soft sheep cheese, and bacon to make the dish called *bryndzove halusky*.

Cabbage in the form of sauerkraut is featured in many dishes, especially *kapustnica* (kah-poost-NEET-sa), a paprika-spiced soup made of sauerkraut, sausage, and dried mushrooms. Dried plums or fresh apples are sometimes added to the soup. Fresh vegetables and salads—while certainly available in the country today—are not typically a part of the traditional cuisine.

Dairy products are much loved in Slovakia, in the form of butter, buttermilk, cream, sour cream, yogurt, and cheeses.

TRADITIONAL MEALS

Many Slovaks begin their day with a home-cooked breakfast that consists of bread, butter and jam, cheese, eggs, ham or sausage, and yogurt, all washed down with tea or coffee. In the cities, commuters stop in

Bratislava has a thriving street food scene. In addition to the usual international fast food places such as McDonald's and Pizza Hut, street vendors offer a wide array of goodies. Sausages are served like hot dogs with loads of toppings. Deep-fried cheese and fried potatoes are also popular. Another favorite street food is *langos*, a crisp, chewy, fried flatbread with sweet or savory toppings.

Flame-grilled sausage, curled from the heat, is served with mustard and a hearty bread. Sausage is a favorite snack, often grilled at picnics and other outdoor activities.

at bakeries, where they enjoy *kolace*, sweet pastries stuffed with fillings like cottage cheese, plum jam, or poppy seeds.

Working people almost always partake of a midmorning refreshment at a street snack bar. The most popular takeout food is the *parok* (PUH-rahk), a sausage that is dipped in mustard or horseradish and served in a white roll. Another favorite is langos (LUHN-gahs), deep-fried dough smothered in garlic butter.

Although the style of cooking may vary somewhat from region to region, lunch and dinner usually begin with *polievko* (PAH-lee-ehv-kah), a hearty soup. The best-known soup is kapustnica, mentioned above. Two other popular soups are *fazulova polievka* (FEH-zoo-lah-vuh PAH-lee-ehv-kuh), a mixture of beans and vegetables, and *cesnakova polievka* (TSEH-snuh-kah-vah PAH-lee-ehv-kuh), a garlic soup in a chicken-broth base with parsley and egg.

The main course is usually a dish based on pork or beef, such as gulas, steak, roasted pork with sauerkraut, pork chops, or spicy meatballs. Less often, roasted chicken, tripe, or trout is prepared. Served with the meat or fish are potatoes, or potato or bread dumplings. Pickled or fresh vegetable salads, as well as cooked vegetables, are traditional side dishes.

FRUITS AND SWEETS

In many rural areas, residents have their own gardens that produce fresh fruit and vegetables during the warmer months. A summer specialty is plum dumplings, made with plums grown in Slovakia. While still warm, the dumplings are sprinkled with poppy seeds that have been mixed with sugar and melted butter.

Other popular desserts are cheese or apple strudel and ice cream. *Makovy kolac* (MUH-kah-vih KAH-luhk), a homemade poppy-seed cake, is another favorite. Walnut rolls (*orechovnik*) are also much loved and can easily be found at any pastry shop. In spa towns, sweet wafers called *kupelne oblatky* (KOO-pehl-neh AH-bluht-kih) are very popular.

For home cooks, a fruit coffee cake called *bublanina* (BOO-blah-NEE-nah) is easy to make for breakfast or dessert. It's usually made with fresh cherries, blueberries, or raspberries, but it can also be made with a variety of other fruits.

In city centers, *trdelnik* (tre-DEL-nyeek; the *r* is trilled), or chimney cake, is a pastry that is often cooked and sold by street vendors. It's not the sort of thing a home cook would make. The sweet dough is wrapped around hot metal cylinders, which spin over glowing coals or another heat source. The baked pastry slides off the spit and is rolled in sugar or cinnamon. Sometimes the trdelnik is served upright like an ice cream cone, filled with fresh fruit, ice cream, or another sweet, creamy filling. This Slovak specialty is also found in the Czech Republic, Hungary, and Austria, and is a favorite with tourists.

Trdelnik, a spiral-wrapped sugared dough, is a traditional sweet often sold on city streets.

VEGETARIAN CHOICES

It may not be easy to be a vegetarian in Slovakia, but it is certainly possible. A traditional vegetarian dish is *vyprazny syr* (VEE-pruh-zhnee SEER), a piece of Edam cheese that is fried in breadcrumbs and served with french fries and tartar sauce. Cheese and potato omelets, fried dumplings with egg, and fried mushrooms with potatoes are the basis of other popular meatless meals. In the larger cities and towns, many restaurant menus now include a section called *bezmasite jedla* (BEHJ-meh-sih-tay YEHD-lah), which literally means "without meat." There's even an annual vegan festival in Bratislava, Veganske Hody.

Fried cheese with french fries and tartar sauce makes for a meatless meal, not exactly common in traditional Slovak cuisine.

BEVERAGES

The legal drinking age in Slovakia is 18. Alcoholic drinks are popular and are consumed at home, in restaurants, and in pubs. Beer is considered to be the national drink of Slovakia.

Slovakia is well known for the plum brandy slivovica, a clear, potent spirit that is aged for three years in oak barrels. *Borovicka* (BAH-rah-vee-kuh), a brandy that tastes like gin, is made in the Spis area from juniper berries. A brandy made from pears in rural areas is also a favorite.

About 2,000 years ago, the ancient Romans brought winemaking to the region that is now Slovakia, and winemaking is still an ongoing tradition. Vineyards and wine production are located primarily in three major areas—the southwest, the expanse between Bratislava and Trnava, and the eastern region near Mala Trna. Slovaks frequently drink locally produced wine with their meals. Many people who live in the countryside make wines and brandies for their own use and give them as gifts.

Mineral water is a widely used nonalcoholic beverage, as few Slovaks drink tap water. Coffee, called *kava* (KAH-vah), is a very strong brew served in small cups. Tea, called *caj*, is a weak beverage taken without milk. Sour milk and *zincica* (ZEEN-tsee-tsuh), a local drink made from sheep's milk, are popular nonalcoholic choices. Slovakia is a market for imported soft drinks from many countries, and they are widely available, as are locally produced fruit juices.

INTERNET LINKS

https://adventurousmiriam.com/food-in-slovakia
This site presents a good introduction to Slovak cuisine, with many photos.

https://theculturetrip.com/europe/slovakia/articles/
10-traditional-slovak-dishes-you-must-try
This page features photos and descriptions of popular Slovak dishes.

KAPUSTNICA (CABBAGE SOUP)

This hearty soup is traditional at Christmastime or New Year's Eve. When served on Christmas Eve, it is sometimes made without meat.

1 pound (450 grams) smoked ham or pork chops

1 pound (450 g) smoked spicy sausage, such as kielbasa

3 quarts (approximately 3 liters) water

1½ ounces (42 grams) dried porcini or shiitake mushrooms

1 32-ounce (ca. 1 kilogram) package sauerkraut, drained and chopped, reserve liquid

1 large onion, chopped

2 bay leaves

6 prunes, pitted and cut in half

1 teaspoon caraway seeds, lightly toasted and chopped

2 teaspoons paprika (sweet, hot, or smoked)

salt, pepper to taste

1 tablesoon sugar, optional

sour cream for serving

Place meat in a large pot with water, and bring to a boil. Cover, and lower heat. Let simmer for 1 hour. Remove meat from the broth, cool, and cut into bite-size pieces.

Meanwhile, soak the mushrooms: In a small bowl, cover mushrooms with cold water, and let soak for 30 minutes. Then drain and chop, and set aside. Discard soaking water.

To the meat broth, add the sauerkraut and its liquid, chopped onion, bay leaves, prunes, mushrooms, caraway, and paprika. Bring to a boil, then lower heat, cover, and simmer for 30 minutes. Remove bay leaves and discard. Stir in the meat, and salt and pepper to taste. Add sugar if desired, to counter sourness. Warm through.

To serve, ladle into bowls, and top with a dollop of sour cream.

BUBLANINA (BUBBLE CAKE)

There are many versions of this homey cake across Slovakia and the Czech Republic. It can also be made with cherries or raspberries.

1¼ cups (300 milliliters) whole milk
5 eggs, yolks and whites separated into two bowls
¼ cup (60 mL) vegetable oil
2 cups flour
¾ cup powdered sugar
1 teaspoon baking powder
1 teaspoon vanilla extract
¼ tsp salt
2 cups fresh blueberries, tossed with 1 tablespoon of flour
powdered sugar, for dusting

Preheat oven to 350°F (175°C).

Prepare a 9×9-inch (23×23-centimeter) pan (or any pan that holds about 2 quarts, or 2 liters, of batter) with baking spray or butter and flour.

In a medium bowl, whisk together the dry ingredients: flour, powdered sugar, baking powder, and salt. Set aside.

In a large bowl, whisk together the milk, egg yolks, and oil until smooth. Whisk in vanilla. Add the dry ingredients to the wet, and mix until smooth.

In a separate large bowl, whip the egg whites until glossy and stiff peaks form.

Using a spatula, fold the egg whites into the batter, a little a time, until the mixture is airy and light. Do not overmix. Some streaks are OK. Add the batter to cake pan, and top with fruit.

Bake for about 30 minutes, or until a toothpick inserted comes out clean.

Cool, sprinkle with powdered sugar (place a couple of tablespoons in a sieve and shake over cake), and cut into squares.

A   B   C   D

POLAND

1

CZECH REPUBLIC

• Zilina

ZILINA

Orava

Liptovsky
Mikulas

▲ *Gerlachovsky Stit
(8,711 ft / 2,655 m)*

2

Vah

• Trencin

TRENCIN

• Poprad   • Levoca

• Uhrovec   • Novaky

*Dumbier
(6,703 ft / 2,043 m)* ▲

Spisska
Nova Ves

• Banska Bystrica

KOSICE

A
U
S
T
R
I
A

Piestany •

TRNAVA

• Trnava

BRATISLAVA

• Modra

Sered •

• BRATISLAVA

• Nitra

NITRA

• Diakovce

• Vyhne   • Zvolen

BANSKA BYSTRICA

• Velky
Krtis

3

Hron

Komarno
•

Dunaj (Danube)

4

━━ International boundary
─── Regional boundary
● Capital city

Feet	Meters
9,900	3,000
6,600	2,000
3,300	1,000
1,650	500
660	200
0	0

N

HUNGARY

Austria, A2—A4

Banska Bystrica, C2
Bardejov, E2
Bratislava, A3

Carpathian Mountains, E1, E2, F1, F2
Czech Republic, A1, A2, B1, B2, C1

Danube River, B4
Diakovce, B3
Dunajec River, D1

Gerlachovsky Stit, D2

Hervartov, E2
Hron River, B3
Humenne, E2
Hungary, A3, A4, B4, C3, C4, D3, D4, E3, E4, F3, F4

Komarno, B4
Kosice, E2

Levoca, D2
Liptovsky Mikulas, C2

Modra, A3

Nitra, B3
Novaky, B2

Piestany, B3
Poland, B1, C1, C2, D1, D2, E1, F1, F2
Poprad, D2
Presov, E2
Prikra, E1

Romania, E4, F3, F4

Sered, B3
Spisska Nova Ves, D2
Svidnik, E2

Trencin, B2
Trnava, A3

Uhrovec, B2
Ukraine, F1—F3

Vah River, B2
Velky Krtis, C3
Vyhne, C2

Zilina, C2
Zvolen, C2

ECONOMIC SLOVAKIA

Agriculture

Corn

Potatoes

Sugar Beets

Vegetables

Wheat

Natural Resources

Coal

Timber

Services

Airport

Port

Tourism

Train Station

Manufacturing

Beer

Cement

Ceramics

Food Products

Machinery

Nuclear Power

Sugar

Textiles

Wine

ABOUT THE ECONOMY

All figures are 2017 estimates unless otherwise noted.

GROSS DOMESTIC PRODUCT (OFFICIAL EXCHANGE RATE)
$95.96 billion

GDP PER CAPITA
$33,100

GDP GROWTH
3.4 percent

GDP COMPOSITION, BY SECTOR OF ORIGIN
agriculture: 3.8 percent
industry: 35 percent
services: 61.2 percent

MINERAL RESOURCES
lignite; small amounts of iron ore, copper and manganese ore; salt

CURRENCY
Euro
1 US dollar = 0.92 euros (February 2020)

AGRICULTURAL PRODUCTS
grains, potatoes, sugar beets, hops, fruit, pigs, cattle, poultry, forest products

INDUSTRIES
automobiles, metal and metal products, electricity, gas, oil, nuclear fuel, chemicals, synthetic fibers, wood and paper products, machinery, earthenware and ceramics, textiles, electrical and optical apparatuses, rubber products, food and beverages, pharmaceuticals

MAJOR EXPORTS
vehicles and parts, machinery, electronic equipment, nuclear reactors and furnaces, iron and steel, mineral oils and fuels (2015)

MAJOR IMPORTS
vehicles and parts, electronic equipment, cars, crude petroleum, petroleum gas (2015)

MAIN TRADE PARTNERS
Germany, Czech Republic, Austria, Poland, Hungary, France, Italy, United Kingdom, South Korea, Russia, China

LABOR FORCE
2.758 million

LABOR FORCE BY OCCUPATION
agriculture: 3.9 percent
industry: 22.7 percent
services: 73.4 percent (2015)

UNEMPLOYMENT RATE
8.1 percent

POPULATION BELOW POVERTY LINE
12.3 percent (2015)

INFLATION RATE
1.3 percent

CULTURAL SLOVAKIA

Piestany
People visit this spa town on the Vah River for its healing hot springs and mud baths.

Vychodna Folklore Festival
Folk arts groups perform Slovak customs, songs, and dances wearing traditional clothing in this three-day July event in the High Tatras region.

Carthusian Monastery
The Cerveny Klastor ("Red Monastery"), with its original Gothic church, located at the mouth of the Dunajec Gorge, was established in 1319. The site is now a museum.

Bardejov
This World Heritage site is a perfectly preserved medieval city with fortified walls, gates, and a town square. The old Jewish complex includes a synagogue and ritual bath.

Bratislava
Among the capital's landmarks are the iconic Bratislava Castle, founded in the 15th century, and the pale pink, 18th-century Primate's Palace, with its famous Hall of Mirrors.

Demanovska Caves
The Demonovska Caves in Low Tatras National Park form Slovakia's longest cave system. The ice cave alone is 5,742 feet (1,750 m) long. The caves are a popular tourist attraction.

Spis Castle
Slovakia's largest castle, located above the town of Spisske Podhradie, was founded in 1209. It is part of a UNESCO World Heritage site.

Wooden Churches
The traditional wooden churches of eastern Slovakia were built without the use of nails. The Church of Saint Francis of Assisi in Hervatov is the country's oldest, built around 1500. It is decorated with frescoes and is one of eight structures that form a UNESCO World Heritage site.

ABOUT THE CULTURE

All figures are 2020 estimates unless otherwise noted.

OFFICIAL NAME
Slovenska Republica (Slovak Republic)
conventional short form: Slovakia

FLAG DESCRIPTION
three equal horizontal bands of white, blue, and red, superimposed with the Slovak cross in a shield; the cross is white on a background of red and blue

TOTAL AREA
18,933 square miles (49,035 square km)

CAPITAL
Bratislava

POPULATION
5,440,602

POPULATION GROWTH RATE
-0.05 percent

URBANIZATION
urban population: 53.8 percent of total population
rate of urbanization: 0 percent annual rate of change

ETHNIC GROUPS
Slovak 80.7 percent, Hungarian 8.5 percent, Roma 2 percent, other 1.8 percent (includes Czech, Ruthenian, Ukrainian, Russian, German, Polish), unspecified 7 percent (2011)
Note: Data represents population by nationality; Roma populations are usually underestimated in official statistics and may represent 7 to 11 percent of Slovakia's population.

RELIGIONS
Roman Catholic 62 percent, Protestant 8.2 percent, Greek Orthodox 3.8 percent, other or unspecified 12.5 percent, none 13.4 percent (2011)

MAIN LANGUAGES
Slovak (official) 78.6 percent, Hungarian 9.4 percent, Romani 2.3 percent, Ruthenian 1 percent, other or unspecified 8.8 percent (2011)

LIFE EXPECTANCY AT BIRTH
total population: 77.8 years
male: 74.3 years
female: 81.6 years

TIMELINE

IN SLOVAKIA	IN THE WORLD
833–907	
The Slav empire of Great Moravia exists.	**1000**
1018	The Chinese perfect gunpowder and
Slovakia becomes part of Greater Hungary.	begin to use it in warfare.
1526	
Upper Hungary (Slovakia) is	**1620**
seized by the Habsburg dynasty.	Pilgrims sail the *Mayflower* to America.
	1776
1867	The US Declaration of Independence is signed.
The Austro-Hungarian monarchy is formed.	**1869**
Magyarization is carried out in Slovakia.	The Suez Canal opens.
1907	
Hungarian becomes the official and	**1914**
only legal language of Slovakia.	World War I begins.
1918	
The Austro-Hungarian Empire falls.	
Slovakia, Ruthenia, Bohemia, and Moravia	
form independent Czechoslovakia.	
1938	
Following the Munich Agreement, Slovakia	
declares itself an autonomous state.	
1939	**1939–1945**
Slovakia becomes an ally of Nazi Germany.	World War II devastates Europe.
1944	
The Slovak National Uprising takes place.	
1945	**1945**
The Czechoslovakian government is	The North Atlantic Treaty Organization
established at Kosice as the war winds down.	(NATO) is formed.
1948	
Communists take over Czechoslovakia.	
	1957
	The Russians launch *Sputnik*.
	1966–1969
1968	The Chinese Cultural Revolution takes place.
The Prague Spring sees reforms. Soviet troops	**1969**
march into Czechoslovakia to stop the rebellion.	US astronaut Neil Armstrong becomes
	the first human on the moon.
	1981
	The AIDS epidemic begins.

IN SLOVAKIA		IN THE WORLD
		1986
		The Chernobyl nuclear power disaster takes place.
1989		**1991**
The Velvet Revolution topples communism.		The Soviet Union breaks up.
1992		
The Slovak parliament votes for independence.		
Vladimir Meciar is elected prime minister.		
1993		
The Velvet Divorce: Slovakia becomes an independent country.		
1994–1998		**1997**
Meciar passes antidemocratic laws that draw heavy international criticism.		Britain returns Hong Kong to China.
1998		
Mikulas Dzurinda is elected prime minister.		**2001**
1998–2002		9/11 terrorist attacks take place in the United States.
Slovakia suffers poor economic performance, high unemployment, and ethnic tensions.		**2003**
		The War in Iraq begins.
2004		
Slovakia joins the European Union.		**2008**
		The United States elects its first African American president, Barack Obama.
2009		**2009**
Slovakia joins the Eurozone, adopting the euro as its currency.		Outbreak of H1N1 flu spreads around the world.
2012		
Robert Fico becomes prime minister.		
2015		**2015–2016**
Fico opposes EU migrant quotas.		ISIS launches terror attacks in Belgium and France.
		2017
2018		Donald Trump becomes US president.
Journalist Jan Kuciak and fiancée Martina Kusnirova are murdered; Fico resigns.		Hurricanes devastate Texas, Caribbean islands, and Puerto Rico.
2019		**2019**
Pro-EU candidate Zuzana Caputova becomes president.		Notre Dame Cathedral in Paris is damaged by fire. Donald Trump is impeached.
2020		**2020**
Parliamentary elections bring populist Igor Matovic to power as prime minister.		A coronavirus epidemic spreads throughout the world.

GLOSSARY

Action K
The Communist Party's attempt, in 1950, to dismantle the Catholic Church in Czechoslovakia.

atheism
The doctrine that there is no deity. This was the only moral doctrine permitted under communism.

bryndzove halusky
The Slovak national dish, consisting of potato dumplings with sheep's cheese and bacon.

Czechoslovakia
The Central European country (1918—1992) that was divided in January 1993 into the separate countries of Slovakia and the Czech Republic.

European Union (EU)
The organization of European countries dedicated to increasing economic integration and strengthening cooperation among its members. Slovakia joined the European Union on May 1, 2004.

Führer
A German word meaning "leader" or "guide," especially a tyrant. Adolf Hitler took the title to establish his absolute authority over Germany. Since then, the word has been associated almost exclusively with Hitler.

fujara (FOO-yuh-ruh)
A 6-foot-long (1.8 m) traditional flute played at folk performances in Slovakia.

Hlinka
The pro-Nazi Slovak People's Party during World War II.

Magyarization
Hungarianization; the program by the Austro-Hungarian Empire aimed at eliminating Slovak culture and language.

Roma
A nomadic people originally from northern India; they were formerly known as Gypsies, though the term is now considered offensive.

slivovica (SLEE-vah-vee-kuh)
Plum brandy.

spelunker
One who explores caves.

Velvet Revolution
The six-week period in 1989, between November 17 and December 29, during which mass demonstrations brought about the bloodless overthrow of the Czechoslovakian Communist Party regime.

FOR FURTHER INFORMATION

BOOKS

DK Eyewitness Travel. *Czech and Slovak Republics.* New York, NY: DK Publishing, 2018.

Edwards, Brendan. *Culture Smart! Slovakia.* London, UK: Kuperand, 2011.

MacDonagh-Pajerova, Monika, et al. *The Velvet Revolution: 30 Years After.* Prague, Czech Republic: Karolinum Press, Charles University, 2020.

Mallows, Lucy, and Tim Burford. *Bratislava.* Chalfont St. Peter, UK: Bradt Travel Guides, 2020.

Spiesz, Anton, and Dusan Caplovic. *Illustrated Slovak History: A Struggle for Sovereignty in Central Europe.* Wauconda, IL: Bolchazy-Carducci Publishers, Inc., 2006.

ONLINE

BBC News. "Slovakia Country Profile." http://news.bbc.co.uk/2/hi/europe/country_profiles/ 1108491.stm.

CIA. *The World Factbook.* "Slovakia." https://www.cia.gov/library/publications/the-world-factbook/geos/lo.html.

Culture Trip. "Slovakia." https://theculturetrip.com/europe/slovakia.

Encyclopedia Britannica. "Slovakia." https://www.britannica.com/place/Slovakia.

Slovak Spectator. https://spectator.sme.sk.

UNESCO World Heritage Convention. "Slovakia." https://whc.unesco.org/en/statesparties/sk.

MUSIC

Slovak Radio Symphony Orchestra. *Alexander Moyzes: Dances from Slovakia,* Naxos, 2019.

String Ensemble of the Slovak Sinfonietta Zilina. *Archi Di Slovakia,* Pavlik Records, 2007.

Urpin Folklore Ensemble. *Slovakia Songs and Dances,* ARC Music, 2010.

FILM

Slovakia: Treasures in the Heart of Europe. Directed by Pat Uskert. Janson Media, 2016.

Touring the World's Capital Cities: Bratislava. Directed by Frank Ullman. TravelVideoStore.com, 2014.

BIBLIOGRAPHY

Accace. "2020 Tax Guideline for Slovakia." https://accace.com/tax-guideline-for-slovakia/#:~:text=.

BBC News. "Slovakia Country Profile." http://news.bbc.co.uk/2/hi/europe/country_profiles/1108491.stm.

BBC News. "Slovakia Profile—Timeline." https://www.bbc.com/news/world-europe-17848213.

Caverle, Romy, and Marijn Butter. "No Place for the Modern Feminist in Traditional Slovakia." *International Angle*, May 28, 2019. https://theinternationalangle.com/index.php/2019/05/28/no-place-for-the-modern-feminist-in-traditional-slovakia.

CIA. *The World Factbook*. "Slovakia." https://www.cia.gov/library/publications/the-world-factbook/geos/lo.html.

Economist Intelligence Unit. *Democracy Index 2019*. http://www.eiu.com/Handlers/WhitepaperHandler.ashx?fi=Democracy-Index-2019.pdf&mode=wp&campaignid=democracyindex2019.

Encyclopedia Britannica. "Slovakia." https://www.britannica.com/place/Slovakia.

Eurofound. "Living and Working in Slovakia." https://www.eurofound.europa.eu/country/slovakia#survey-results.

Gosling, Tim. "Slovakia Seeks Escape from Corruption Black Hole." *Al Jazeera*, February 28, 2020. https://www.aljazeera.com/news/2020/02/slovakia-seeks-escape-corruption-black-hole-200226135428581.html.

Helliwell, John F., Richard Layard, Jeffrey Sachs, and Jan-Emmanuel De Neve, eds. 2020. *World Happiness Report 2020*. New York, NY: Sustainable Development Solutions Network. https://worldhappiness.report.

Santora, Marc, and Miroslava Germanova. "Slovak Businessman Charged with Ordering Murder of Journalist Jan Kuciak." *New York Times*, March 14, 2019. https://www.nytimes.com/2019/03/14/world/europe/slovakia-jan-kuciak-kocner.html.

Shift Team. "Kuciak Family Immediately Suspected Businessman Marian Kocner." *Shift News*, January 16, 2020. https://theshiftnews.com/2020/01/16/kuciak-family-immediately-suspected-businessman-marian-kocner.

Starr, Kelsey Jo. "Once the Same Nation, the Czech Republic and Slovakia Look Very Different Religiously." Fact Tank, Pew Research Center, January 2, 2019. https://www.pewresearch.org/fact-tank/2019/01/02/once-the-same-nation-the-czech-republic-and-slovakia-look-very-different-religiously.

US Department of State. "Slovak Republic 2018 International Religious Freedom Report." https://www.state.gov/wp-content/uploads/2019/05/SLOVAKIA-2018-INTERNATIONAL-RELIGIOUS-FREEDOM-REPORT.pdf.

World Jewish Congress. "Slovakia." https://www.worldjewishcongress.org/en/about/communities/SK.

INDEX

INDEX